DATE DUE

Best recipes from the backs of boxes, bottles, cans and jars

Best recipes from the backs of boxes, bottles, cans and jars

by Ceil Dyer

McGraw-Hill Book Company

New York   St. Louis   San Francisco
Toronto   Düsseldorf   Mexico

Printed in the United States of America.
No part of this publication may be reproduced, stored in a retrieval system, or transmitted, in any form or by any means, electronic, mechanical, photo-copying, recording, or otherwise, without the prior written permission of the publisher. Many of the trademarks used in this book are registered with the U.S. Patent Office and may not be used without permission.

1 2 3 4 5 6 7 8 9 0 FGRFGR 7 8 3 2 1 0 9

LIBRARY OF CONGRESS CATALOGING IN PUBLICATION DATA
Dyer, Ceil.
  Best recipes from the backs of boxes, bottles, cans, and jars.
  1. Cookery.   I. Title.
TX715.D9772   641.5   79-17925
ISBN 0-07-018551-4
ISBN 0-07-018550-6 pbk.

Book design by Marsha Picker.

Contents

We wish to thank the following for permission to use these recipes:

Castle and Cooke, Inc.
Thomas J. Lipton, Inc.
Best Foods, a Division of CPC
    International, Inc.
American Pop Corn Company
    (JOLLY TIME Pop Corn)
Elam's
Kellogg Company
Purity Cheese Company
Duffy-Mott Company, Inc.
Stokely-Van Camp, Inc.
Dannon Milk Products
Seafood Marketing Authority
California Almond Growers
    Exchange
Holland House Brands Co.
William J. Underwood Company
Old El Paso Foods
Heinz U.S.A., a Division of The H. J.
    Heinz Co.
Frito-Lay, Inc.
The California Avocado Advisory
    Board, Inc.
Ac´cent International, Inc.
Bacardi Imports, Inc.
Kraft, Inc.
Swift & Co.
Progresso Quality Foods
Ralston Purina Company
Sunkist Growers, Inc.

Campbell's Soup Company
Hiram Walker & Sons, Inc.
Apricot Advisory Board
Oscar Mayer & Co.
McIlhenny Co.
Armour Food Co.
Cointreau Liqueur, Ltd.
Pillsbury BAKE-OFF®
Delmarva Poultry Industry, Inc.
C. F. Mueller Co.
Tyson Foods, Inc.
Brooke Bond Foods, Inc.
R. T. French Company
Pet, Inc.
Standard Brands
General Foods Corporation
International Multifoods
AmStar, Inc.
Libby, McNeill & Libby, Inc.
Borden, Inc.
Hershey Foods Corp.
Standard Milling Company
Hunt-Wesson Foods, Inc.
Gerber Products Company
Quaker Oats Company
The Nestle Company, Inc.
Uncle Ben's, Inc.
Amaretto di Saronno
Riviana Foods
Del Monte Corp.

Introduction

This is in essence *your* book—or, to put it more accurately, the cookbook you would have undoubtedly compiled if only you had time for the project. For here are the recipes you meant to save from that jar, can or box top, recipes you and your friends have asked for, a good number your mother's generation requested, and even a few of your grandmother's choices. Recipes you meant to save but didn't, those from magazine ads you may have torn out intending to file away someday, but that someday never came. In short, here is the cookbook you have always wanted: a treasury of the very best efforts of America's food producers.

In compiling this book I have come to appreciate how really lucky we are in this country; not only do we have an abundance of food, we are rich in the variety and quality of food produced and distributed to us by our food companies. It is apparently not enough for a company to sell a can of beets; they must be the best beets obtainable. Grown especially for the packer, they are superior to begin with. They must then be expertly canned for maximum flavor and best texture. Nor does the effort to get a good product to your table end there; a team of good cooks goes to work to create new and delicious ways for you to serve those beets; testing and retesting until they are satisfied the results are letter-perfect and that you, the customer, will be pleased. Flour millers, sugar refiners, convenience food producers, meat packers, canners and purveyors of spices, sauces and dressings, all give time and effort in abundance to produce not just good food, but to give you the best possible way to cook and serve their products. No other industry tries harder to please you; after all, do automobile makers offer to teach you to drive? Does the maker of carpets give expert professional decorating service? But the food people! Virtual armies of talented home economists, chefs and just plain good cooks labor long and hard to create recipes that are not only good, but perfect, time after time after time.

As anyone knows, the measure of a good cookbook is the absolute reliability of the recipes; almost anyone with a little knowledge of food can *write* a good recipe, but one that can be depended upon for uniformly good results is the only one that counts in the kitchen.

Good recipes, plain-jane or fancy, are the result of testing; making the casserole, stew or cake from scratch under average home kitchen conditions, then doing it over and over again until every detail is crystal-clear and the results are uniformly perfect.

Good recipes are also those that offer a new food idea, new combinations that perhaps you haven't thought of before; but that too requires testing and experimenting. Not every food "love affair" ends in a happy "marriage." A good idea is only as good as it looks and tastes, and that means trying out idea after idea until indeed the recipe is as good as it sounds. For the truth is that all good cookbooks are written at the kitchen counter, not at the typewriter; and, while the poet may find inspiration in a sunset, cookbook writers must find theirs at the stove. I have sifted through over fifteen hundred recipes from different sources to select the best, you may be sure that every one will be a success, a can't-fail predictable success, every time you make it. America's best cooks have made certain of that.

Happy cooking!

1.

Appetizers

That "something before" or the hospitable hors d'oeuvre, be it for a casual "stop by for a drink" or a full-blown cocktail party, is ever a challenge. Too much or too heavy is too bad, too little a disappointment, but have no qualms, for easy delicious "starters" are at hand from the good cooks who contributed their best to this book.

These talented people also passed along a few tips for a successful cocktail party that can be useful to any host or hostess. I include them here for your pleasure. . . .

An electric wok, usually available in handsome colors, is a very useful substitute for a chafing dish. In my opinion, it is a bit more dependable and requires less watching.

Serve a variety of breads, toasts and crackers; remember, cheese and highly flavored spreads and pâtés are at their best when the breads or crackers are not too highly flavored. Choose thin slices of cocktail rye, rounds of French or Italian loaves, homemade melba toast made from thin white bread, unsalted water biscuits and the like. Too much seasoning in the crackers ruins the cook's efforts.

Do serve raw vegetables for dipping. Try celery stalks, carrot sticks, thin slices of turnip, apple, cauliflowerets, endive stalks and the like—great for flavor, and the calorie-conscious will love you.

Do, please do, have plenty of ice, loads of it; nothing cools off a party like warm drinks.

Serve enough! People like to munch at a party, and even a small gathering can consume an amazing amount of food. Endless variety isn't necessary, but whatever you serve it should be plentiful.

If you are a "helpless" host or hostess it pays to set up a buffet where people can help themselves. A bar tray with a generous ice bucket will probably occupy one end of the table, with a chafing dish or wok holding the stage at the other. Cold dips, cheeses and spreads make up the balance of the array.

Avoid cocktail foods that require individual serving plates; fork foods too are out unless you have help at hand to gather up the remains. The best advice for all but very formal occasions is: stick to finger foods.

Do have plenty of cocktail napkins. Paper ones are definitely okay; there are very attractive ones available, but have lots of them. Nothing is worse than needing a napkin at a party and finding none available.

The important thing is to have a good time. The recipes included here should certainly assure you of that. Great-tasting, easy, imaginative, they are from some of the best cooks in the business. I am certain you will enjoy every one.

Party Cheese Ball

We couldn't put together a cookbook of favorite recipes without Philadelphia Cream Cheese, the all-time star of the appetizer tray.

2 8-ounce packages
  Philadelphia Brand
  Cream Cheese
2 8-ounce cups shredded
  Cracker Barrel sharp
  Cheddar cheese
1 Tbs. chopped pimiento
1 Tbs. chopped green
  pepper

1 Tbs. finely chopped
  onion
2 tsp. Worcestershire
  sauce
1 tsp. lemon juice
  Dash of cayenne
  Dash of salt
  Finely chopped pecans

Combine softened cream cheese and Cheddar cheese, mixing until well blended. Add pimiento, green pepper, onion, Worcestershire sauce, lemon juice and seasonings; mix well. Chill. Shape into ball; roll in nuts. Serve with crackers.

During the party season, leftover cheese ball can be reshaped and refrigerated until the next event. Will keep up to one week.

Roast Beef Party Snacks

This great idea is from the Underwood Red Devil Roast Beef Spread label.

12–15 melba rounds
1 (4¾ ounces) can
  Underwood Roast Beef
  Spread

½ cup grated Cheddar
  cheese
1 Tbs. minced onion

Spread melba round with roast beef spread. Top with grated cheese and minced onion. Broil for 3 to 5 minutes or until cheese bubbles. Makes 12–15 snacks.

From Heinz

Pick Pockets

Mix well 2 cups finely grated American cheese, ½ cup softened butter or margarine. Using pastry blender, cut in 1 cup all-purpose flour, dash cayenne. Divide into 2 balls; chill. Cut 36 strips (2 × ½-inch) from Heinz Dill or Sweet Pickles. Roll each ball to ⅛-inch thickness on floured board; cut in rectangles (2½ × 2-inch). Wrap a pickle strip in dough; seal ends well. Place on ungreased baking sheets. Bake in 425°F. oven, 12 to 15 minutes. Makes 3 dozen.

Dill Fondue Balls

Combine 2 slightly beaten egg whites, 1 cup grated Swiss cheese, ⅓ cup chopped Heinz Dills, dash garlic salt. Drop by teaspoonsful into ½ cup dry bread crumbs; roll and coat well, forming small balls. Chill until ready to serve. Fry in deep fat (375°F.) until golden brown, 2 to 3 minutes. Drain on absorbent paper. Makes 2 dozen appetizers.

Peppy Bean Dip

An easy great and money-saving appetizer from the Old El Paso Refried Beans can.

1 (16-ounces) can Old El
Paso Refried Beans
1 cup dairy sour cream
3 to 5 Old El Paso Pickled
jalapeño peppers seeded
and rinsed

Shredded Cheddar
cheese
Sliced green onion
Old El Paso Tostada
Shells, broken

Blend together refried beans and sour cream. Finely chop the jalapeño peppers; mix well with bean mixture. Spoon into serving bowl; garnish with shredded Cheddar cheese and sliced green onion, if desired. Serve with broken tostada shells for dippers. Makes 2¾ cups.

Chippy Cheese Ball

This is an especially good cheese ball to make for your next party. Frito-Lay's test kitchen director tells us it improves with chilling, so it's easy to make ahead and store in your refrigerator or freezer. (Note: if you place it in the freezer be sure to defrost completely before serving.)

1 lb. sharp Cheddar
cheese, grated
¼ lb. Roquefort cheese,
crumbled
½ lb. cream cheese
2 tsps. Worcestershire
sauce

2 Tbs. grated onion
¼ tsp. cayenne pepper
1¼ cups crushed Lay's
Brand Sour Cream &
Onion Flavored Potato
Chips

Have cheeses at room temperature. Blend well with mixer or pastry blender. Add Worcestershire sauce, onion, pepper, and ¼ cup of the crushed Lay's Brand Sour Cream & Onion Flavored Potato Chips. Shape into ball and roll in remaining chips until completely covered. Chill well.

Deviled Ham Stuffed Cucumbers

A perfect appetizer from Underwood; easy, great-tasting, low in calories and light on the budget. Could you ask for more?

2 medium cucumbers
1 4½-ounce can
   Underwood Deviled Ham
1 hard-cooked egg,
   coarsely chopped

1 Tbs. finely chopped
   onion
1 Tbs. finely chopped sour
   pickle
1 tsp. prepared mustard

Cut cucumbers in half lengthwise and scoop out seeds. In a bowl, mix together deviled ham, chopped egg, onion, pickle and mustard. Spoon mixture into cucumber shells. Chill. When ready to serve, cut cucumber diagonally into 1-inch pieces. Makes about 2 dozen hors d'oeuvres.

Guacamole With Green Chili Peppers

More people write to the Avocado Advisory Board for this classic recipe than almost any they have printed during the past decade. Serve with toasted tortillas as a cocktail dip or with tomatoes and Boston lettuce as an appetizer.

4 avocados, mashed or
   puréed
½ cup finely chopped
   canned green chili
   peppers

¼ cup minced onion
1 tsp. salt
½ cup lemon juice

Combine ingredients. Cover and chill. Makes 3 cups.

Mushroom Liver Pâté

Underwood created this luxurious-tasting pâté for your next party. Make it ahead and chill well; it tastes even better the day after it's made.

2 Tbs. butter or margarine
⅔ cup chopped fresh mushrooms
⅓ cup chopped onion
2 cans (4¾-ounce) Underwood Liverwurst Spread

2 Tbs. brandy
2 tsps. dried chives
½ tsp. Ac'cent flavor enhancer

Melt butter in a skillet over medium low heat. Add mushrooms and onions; sauté 10 minutes, until all moisture has evaporated. Stir in liverwurst spread, brandy, chives and flavor enhancer. Spoon into a serving bowl. Chill. Serve cold with crackers. Makes 1½ cups spread.

Eggplant Spread

Here's a sophisticated vegetable appetizer from Ac'cent. Serve it on crisp melba toast.

1 large eggplant (2 lbs.)
1 cup chopped onion
⅓ cup chopped celery
⅓ cup chopped green pepper
2 cloves garlic, finely chopped
¼ cup vegetable oil
2 medium tomatoes, peeled and chopped

1 tsp. Ac'cent flavor enhancer
1 tsp. salt
¼ tsp. ground black pepper
2 Tbs. lemon juice
1 loaf (8-ounces) party rye bread

Preheat oven to 425°F. Bake eggplant on rack in the center of oven 1 hour, until soft. In a large saucepan over low heat, sauté onions, celery, green pepper and garlic in oil for 10 minutes. Remove skin from cooled baked eggplant and finely chop the pulp. Add chopper pulp to the onion mixture and stir in tomatoes, Ac'cent, salt and pepper. Bring mixture to a boil, stirring constantly, reduce heat, cover and simmer 1 hour. Remove cover and cook 30 minutes longer, stirring occasionally. Stir in lemon juice. Refrigerate 3 hours. Serve chilled with party rye bread. Makes 3 cups.

Lipton California Dip

Here's the recipe that started all those great cocktail dips; perfect for parties. Make as much or as little as you need in minutes. It's been going strong since 1954.

In small bowl blend 1 envelope Lipton Onion Soup Mix with 2 cups (16 ounces) sour cream; chill. Makes about 2 cups dip. *Variations:*

California Vegetable Dip: Add 1 green pepper, chopped; 1 tomato, chopped; and 2 tsp. chili powder.

California Blue Cheese Dip: Add ¼ lb. blue cheese, crumbled, and ¼ cup finely chopped walnuts.

California Shrimp Dip: Add 1 cup finely chopped cooked shrimp and ¼ cup catsup.

California Clam Dip: Add 1 can (7½ ounces) minced clams, drained, and 2 Tbs. chili sauce.

Who knows how to give a better party than the light-hearted people at Bacardi Rum down in Miami? Here are four great hors d'oeuvres from their national advertising. Mix up a bunch of Daiquiris and the party is on!

Chicken Liver Dip

Cut ½ lb. chicken livers into small pieces. Melt 2 Tbs. butter or margarine with 1 clove pressed or minced garlic. Sauté livers till cooked through. Remove from heat. Stir in 3 Tbs. Bacardi Dark Rum.* Cool. Combine mixture in a blender with 1 package (8 ounces) softened cream cheese, ¼ cup plain yogurt, ½ tsp. salt, ¼ tsp. crumbled basil. Blend smooth. Salt and pepper to taste. Chill several hours. Serve with crackers and/or raw vegetable pieces. Makes about 1⅓ cups.

Liverwurst Spread

Mash 1 package (8 ounces) liverwurst with fork. Mix in 4 slices cooked crumbled bacon, 1 Tbs. snipped chives, 1 Tbs. Bacardi Dark Rum,* 3 Tbs. softened butter or margarine. Serve with melba toast or crisp crackers. Makes 1 cup.

Sautéed Shrimp

Marinate 1½ lbs. medium shrimp, shelled and deveined, in ½ cup Bacardi Light Rum* several hours. Melt ¼ cup butter or margarine in large frying pan. Add shrimp and rum mixture with ½ tsp. garlic salt. Sauté 8 to 10 minutes or until shrimp cook through. Sprinkle ⅓ cup grated Parmesan cheese and ground pepper over shrimp. Broil 2 to 3 minutes or until cheese browns. Serve hot. Makes about 36 servings.

Mini Meat Balls

Combine 1½ Tbs. Bacardi Light Rum,* 2 Tbs. soy sauce, 1 pressed garlic clove and 1 tsp. ground ginger; blend. Add 1 lb. ground beef chuck. Blend well. Shape into balls about 1 inch in diameter. Bake at 300°F., 12 to 15 minutes, turning once. Serve with wooden picks.

Hot Crabmeat Appetizer

Kraft terms this scrumptious concoction one of their classics. I call it a short cut to becoming the hostess with the mostest. Nobody, but nobody, can resist it!

1 8-ounce package Philadelphia Brand Cream Cheese
1½ cups (7½-ounce can) flaked drained crabmeat
2 Tbs. finely chopped onion

2 Tbs. milk
½ tsp. cream-style horseradish
¼ tsp. salt
Dash of pepper
⅓ cup sliced almonds, toasted

Combine softened cream cheese, crabmeat, onion, milk, horseradish and seasonings, mixing until well blended. Spoon into 9-inch pie plate or oven-proof dish; sprinkle with nuts. Bake at 375°F. 15 minutes. Serve as a dip or a spread with crackers, chips or raw vegetables. Makes about 2 cups.

* Unless otherwise specified all recipes suggesting use of Bacardi Light or Dark Rum refer only to 80-proof rum.

Sausage and Hot Mustard Sauce

In 1965 Swift & Co. printed this recipe, Brown 'N Serve Sausages with Hot Mustard Sauce, on their sausage package. For well over ten years people have consistently asked for the recipe.

1 8-ounce package Swift
   Premium Brown 'N Serve
   Sausage, any flavor

Cut sausage links in halves. Brown according to package directions. Keep hot on hot tray or in chafing dish. Spear sausage pieces with smooth toothpicks. Serve with Hot Mustard Sauce for dipping. Makes 20 appetizers.

Hot Mustard Sauce

2 Tbs. butter or margarine
1 Tbs. flour
½ tsp. salt
1 cup water
1 beef bouillon cube
⅓ cup Dijon-style mustard
2 tsps. horseradish
2 Tbs. sugar

Melt butter in a saucepan. Stir in flour and salt. Gradually add water. Add bouillon cube, mustard, horseradish and sugar. Stir and cook until sauce thickens. Makes 1½ cups.

QUICK AND EASY APPETIZERS

These are some great ideas for "made-in-a-minute" appetizers from Kraft.

- Marinate cooked shrimp in Kraft Italian Dressing for several hours in the refrigerator. Drain and arrange on picks with pitted ripe olives.
- Spread thin ham slices with Philadelphia Brand Whipped Cream Cheese. Roll up and chill. Cut into 1¼-inch pieces.
- Marinate fresh mushroom caps and frozen cooked artichoke hearts in Kraft Caesar Dressing for several hours in the refrigerator. Drain and serve on picks.
- Spread thin slices of French bread with soft margarine. Top with Kraft Shredded Mozzarella Cheese. Heat at 350° until cheese melts.
- Combine flaked crabmeat with enough Kraft Real Mayonnaise to moisten. Season lightly with curry powder. Serve as a spread with melba toast or sesame crackers.
- Serve melon balls, pineapple chunks and apple wedges as dippers with Kraft Blue Cheese Sour Cream Dip.
- Spread one 8-ounce package Philadelphia Brand Cream Cheese with chutney and serve with crackers.
- Stuff large mushroom caps with Philadelphia Brand Whipped Cream Cheese blended with bacon and horseradish, chives or onions.
- Simmer cocktail sausages, ham or luncheon meat cubes in Kraft barbecue sauce. Keep warm in chafing dish or over a warmer.
- Sauté shrimp or scallops in Parkay margarine. Season with dill weed. Serve in chafing dish or over a warmer.

Antipasto for Eight

Progresso Foods suggests this Roman-style appetizer for a buffet supper or cocktail party.

¼ lb. each prosciutto, salami, ham

2 2-ounce cans Progresso Anchovy Fillets

1 large can Progresso Tuna Fish

1 15-ounce can Progresso Artichoke Hearts in Brine, drained

1 7½-ounce can Progresso Caponata

1 jar Progresso Olive Condite or Olive Appetizer

¼ jar Progresso Tuscan Peppers

1 jar Progresso Roasted Peppers

1 can Progresso Giant Ripe Olives

1 jar Progresso Pepper Salad

Sliced tomatoes

celery hearts, cut in halves lengthwise

2 or 3 hard-cooked eggs, cut in quarters

Progresso Pure Olive Oil

Progresso Pure Wine Vinegar

Use a large round platter or lazy susan. Arrange tuna fish in center and surround with all other ingredients, forming a pretty pattern. Serve with cruets of olive oil and vinegar for individual seasoning.

Party Mix

Ralson Purina tells me that this is their long-time, all-time favorite. First record of it in the Checkerboard Kitchens files goes back to 1952.

6 Tbs. butter or margarine

1 tsp. seasoned salt

4 tsps. Worcestershire sauce

2 cups Corn Chex cereal

2 cups Rice Chex cereal

2 cups Wheat Chex cereal

¾ cup salted mixed nuts

Preheat oven to 250°F. Heat butter in 13 × 9 × 2-inch baking pan in oven until melted. Remove. Stir in seasoned salt and Worcestershire sauce. Add Chex and nuts. Mix until all pieces are coated. Heat in oven 45 minutes. Stir every 15 minutes. Spread on absorbent paper to cool. Makes 6¾ cups.

Note: Party Mix may be frozen, so make a double batch. Thaw at room temperature in container in which it was stored.

2.
Main Dishes:
Meat,
Chicken
and Fish

Everyday breakfast has a way of planning itself; lunch, unless it's a party, depends on the day's activity—a sandwich or some soup usually will do; but dinner is important. As it is often the only time the family gets together at the table, it should mark a pleasant end of the day, and it should taste great. America's best cooks wielding their skillets and saucepans in the test kitchens of food companies across the country know this, for they have come up with an almost endless variety of main dishes to please literally every taste, suit every pocketbook and fit every occasion from informal supper to the most elegant party. From "beans and franks" to Rock Cornish game hens stuffed with wild rice, they run the gamut of main dishes from all over the world. Pick a cuisine, any cuisine, and there is a recipe to suit your fancy. Perhaps a Chinese-inspired dish tonight? Or would you prefer an Italian specialty, or German sauerbraten? Perhaps you're in the mood for a Mexican feast. No matter, there's a tried and true recipe here, whatever your preference.

Nor have All-American favorites been overlooked: great meat loaves and casseroles, chicken with gravy, crispy fried fish, or a perfect salmon loaf are main-course "stars."

The really beautiful part of every recipe is its absolute certainty of success. Tested and retested, each recipe has been perfected until it is super-easy, fast and dependable. You will spend less time preparing a really enjoyable dinner, more time in the enjoying—that I can promise you.

In compiling this chapter I have tried to give you a range of main-course recipes to make dinner a pleasurable event. There are recipes to fit each season of the year, every night of the week, whether it be "end of the month" budget or a festive gathering of guests. Light the candles and have a good time—the best part of the day is at hand.

West Coast Broiled Flank Steak

Out in California, the Sunkist Lemon Growers tell me, this is the only way to broil a steak.

1 flank steak, about 1½ pounds
1 onion, thinly sliced
1 tsp. fresh grated lemon peel
½ cup fresh squeezed lemon juice
2 Tbs. sugar
½ tsp. salt
½ tsp. oregano, crushed
⅛ tsp. coarse black pepper
2 Tbs. soy sauce
1 Tbs. butter

Trim any fat or membrane from steak. With knife, score steak ⅛ inch deep on both sides in diamond design. Layer half of onions in plastic bag or glass dish. Place steak on top of onions, cover with remaining onion. Thoroughly combine remaining ingredients except butter; pour over steak and onions. Marinate 2 to 3 hours or overnight in refrigerator, turning several times. Remove steak from marinade; wipe partially dry with paper towel. Drain onions and reserve. Place steak on cold broiler pan, 3 to 5 inches from source of heat in preheated broiler. Broil 3 to 5 minutes on each side. Meanwhile, sauté onions in butter until soft. To serve, cut steak across grain in very thin slices; top with onions. Makes 4 servings.

Quick Chinese Pepper Steak

The Ehlers people tell us their favorite package recipe is this easy Chinese pepper steak. You can cook it in minutes in your wok or electric skillet.

1 lb. round steak, cut ½ inch thick
2 Tbs. salad oil
1 medium onion, sliced
1 medium green pepper, sliced

1 envelope Ehlers Au Jus Gravy Mix
¾ cup water
4 tsps. soy sauce
½ tsp. ground ginger
3 cups hot cooked rice

Cut meat in half lengthwise with a sharp knife, then crosswise into thin slices. Cook meat, onion and pepper in skillet in hot oil until meat is browned. Stir in remaining ingredients except rice. Cook 5 minutes, stirring constantly. Serve over rice. Makes 4 servings.

Korean-Style Flank Steak

The secret of this spicy steak recipe is the Karo Dark Corn Syrup. It's different and delicious.

1½–2 lbs. flank steak
¼ cup sesame seeds
¼ cup corn oil
¼ cup soy sauce
¼ cup Karo Dark Corn Syrup

1 small onion, sliced
1 clove garlic, crushed
¼ tsp. black pepper
¼ tsp. ground ginger

Remove tendons and trim steak. Score meat. In shallow baking dish stir together sesame seeds, corn oil, soy sauce, corn syrup, onion, garlic, pepper and ginger. Add steak, turning to coat. Refrigerate, turning once, several hours or overnight. Broil steak about 6 inches from source of heat, turning once, about 8 minutes, or until cooked to desired doneness. Slice steak diagonally and serve immediately. Makes about 6 servings.

Ranchero Supper Stew

Lipton adapted this authentic Texas recipe for their Onion Soup Mix packaging. It's a great spicy meal in one. Serve with hot cornbread for a true ranch-house supper.

2 Tbs. oil	1 cup water
1½ lbs. beef cubes	2 tsps. chili powder
1 envelope Lipton Onion Soup Mix	2 carrots, thinly sliced
	1 green pepper, chopped
2 cans (16 ounces) whole tomatoes, undrained	½ cup celery, thinly sliced
	2 potatoes, diced

In large skillet, heat oil and brown beef; add onion soup mix blended with tomatoes, water, and chili powder. Simmer, stirring occasionally, 30 minutes. Add carrots, green pepper, celery, and potatoes; cook covered 45 minutes or until vegetables are tender and gravy is slightly thickened. Makes about 6 servings.

Horseradish Dressing for Cold Meats

This zippy dressing is a great accompaniment to cold meat. I also recommend it spooned over hot broiled hamburgers.

1 cup Hellmann's Real Mayonnaise (or Best Foods)	1½ Tbs. horseradish
	½ tsp. salt
½ cup buttermilk	⅛ tsp. pepper
2 Tbs. finely chopped green onion	

Combine all ingredients. Cover; chill 1 hour. Serve over slices of beef, tomato and onions. Makes 1⅔ cups.

Red-Hot Stir-Fry

From Dole comes one of the best stir-fry dishes I've ever tried. Serve it with hot with just-cooked thin noodles for a change.

2 large stalks broccoli	2 Tbs. vinegar
1 lb. beef top round	½ tsp. crushed red pepper
¼ cup oil	2 Tbs. cornstarch
1 can (20-ounce) Dole Pineapple Chunks, in syrup	1 cup fresh bean sprouts
	2 Tbs. sesame seeds, toasted
¼ cup soy sauce	

Trim and slice broccoli diagonally. Slice beef in strips across the grain. Heat oil in wok or skillet till very hot. Add broccoli and stir fry 2 to 3 minutes until barely tender. Add beef strips and cook just until brown. Drain pineapple reserving syrup. Mix syrup with soy sauce, vinegar, red pepper and cornstarch. Add pineapple, bean sprouts and sauce mixture to beef. Heat and stir until thickened. Sprinkle with sesame seeds. Serve over rice or noodles if desired. Makes 4 servings.

Mock Sauerbraten

Good German housewives used to spend days making sauerbraten. Ehler Pot Roast Gravy Mix makes it simple and simply delicious with this easy recipe from the back of their Pot Roast Gravy envelope.

1 package (½-ounce) Ehlers Pot Roast Cooking and Gravy Mix	⅛ tsp. ground cloves
	1 3- to 4-lb. pot roast
	4 carrots, quartered
¾ cup water	2 onions, quartered
½ cup dry red wine	¼ to ½ cup sour cream
¼ cup red wine vinegar	¼ cup gingersnap cookie crumbs

Combine gravy mix, water, wine, vinegar and cloves in a 4-quart Dutch oven and stir to blend well. Add pot roast, cover and cook in a preheated 350° oven for 2 hours. Add carrots and onions, cover and cook 1 hour longer. Remove pot from oven and set meat aside on warm platter. Stir sour cream and gingersnap crumbs into sauce. Serve sauce separately. Makes 6 servings.

Note: Leftover meat may be sliced and served cold with Horseradish Dressing.

Spanish Pot Roast

One of the first recipes demonstrated on Kraft's famous "complete meal" television commercials. A great-tasting flavorful one-pot meal. Save leftovers to serve cold with Kraft horseradish.

3- to 4-lb. pot roast	8 small onions
1 8-ounce bottle Kraft Catalina French Dressing	8 small potatoes
	1 cup stuffed green olive slices
¾ cup water	2 Tbs. flour

Brown meat in ¼ cup dressing. Add remaining dressing and ½ cup water. Cover; simmer 2 hours and 15 minutes. Add onions, potatoes and olives; continue simmering 45 minutes, until meat and vegetables are tender. Remove meat and vegetables to warm serving platter. Gradually add remaining ¼ cup water to flour, stirring until well blended. Gradually add flour mixture to hot liquid in pan; cook, stirring constantly, until mixture boils and thickens. Simmer 3 minutes, stirring constantly. Serve with meat and vegetables. Makes 6 to 8 servings.

In 1976 the Uncle Ben's Rice Company held a contest for the best recipe using their Converted Rice, Quick Rice, Long Grain and Wild Rice mixture or Stuff 'n Such Stuffing mix. Here are three of their prize-winning recipes for your collection. Collector's items they surely are. Each one is super-delicious. If you lost the one you clipped and thought you saved, rejoice! Here it is!

Stuffed Beef Ranchero

Family flank steak in a glamorous new dress.

2 1½-lb. flank steaks
3 tsp. instant meat
    tenderizer
1 6-ounce package Uncle
    Ben's Stuff 'n Such
    Traditional Sage Flavor
1 egg, beaten slightly
½ lb. ground pork sausage
1 medium green pepper,
    chopped
½ cup finely chopped
    onion
1 6-ounce jar stuffed
    green olives, sliced
1 10½-ounce can
    condensed beef broth
1 medium ripe tomato,
    chopped
1 Tbs. flour
2 Tbs. cold water

Pound steaks thin enough to stuff and roll easily. Sprinkle both sides of steaks with tenderizer and treat as manufacturer suggests on package label. Prepare Stuff 'n Such according to package directions, using ¾ cup water. Add egg to stuffing; mix well. Cook sausage meat, pepper and onion in skillet until sausage is lightly browned and onion is tender, about 5 minutes. Drain off excess fat. Add olives and sausage mixture to stuffing and mix well. Spread 1½ cups stuffing on each steak. Roll each steak and tie securely with string. Place steaks in a 13½ × 8½-inch baking dish. Pour broth mixed with tomato over steaks. Bake at 350°F. oven for 1 hour or less until meat is tender yet rare, basting occasionally. Place remaining stuffing in aluminum-foil packet and bake for 30 minutes. Cool meat rolls 5 minutes before slicing. Combine flour and cold water; mix until free of lumps. Stir into pan drippings; continue stirring over medium heat until thickened. Serve with additional stuffing and gravy. Makes 8 to 10 servings.

Reuben Croquettes

A completely new flavor for ever-welcome crisp croquettes.

½ cup Uncle Ben's
  Converted Brand Rice
1 1-lb can sauerkraut
1 12-ounce can corned
  beef
¼ cup chopped onion
3 eggs
1 cup shredded Swiss
  cheese
1 tsp. salt

¼ tsp. pepper
2 Tbs. water
1½ cups fine dry
  breadcrumbs
1 cup mayonnaise
⅓ cup milk
¼ cup prepared mustard
4 tsps. lemon juice
  Oil for frying

Cook rice according to package directions for half the basic recipe. Drain sauerkraut very well, pressing out as much liquid as possible. Chop sauerkraut and corned beef very fine. Add onion, 2 eggs, cooked rice, cheese, salt and pepper; mix well. Shape into 18 croquettes or balls, using ¼ cup of mixture for each. Combine remaining egg and water; beat slightly. Roll each croquette in crumbs, then egg mixture, and again in crumbs. Let dry 10 minutes. Fry croquettes in hot shallow oil, 5 to 7 minutes, turning once, or bake in 450°F. oven for 10 minutes, turn and bake 10 minutes longer. Serve with sauce. Makes 18 croquettes or 6 servings.

Sauce: Combine and mix mayonnaise, milk, mustard and lemon juice.

Cheesy Rice Roll-Ups

Delicate crêpes with an elegant wild rice filling.

Crêpes:
¾ cup milk
3 eggs
¼ tsp. salt
¾ cup all-purpose flour
Melted butter or
margarine

Filling:
1 (6-ounce) package
Uncle Ben's Long Grain
and Wild Rice
1 lb. ground lean beef
1 (4-ounce) can sliced
mushrooms, drained

Sauce:
¼ cup butter or
margarine
2 Tbs. all-purpose flour
1 10¾-ounce can
condensed cream of
mushroom soup
1½ cups milk
1 cup shredded process
American cheese

Prepare crêpes. Combine milk, eggs and salt in small mixing bowl; beat slightly. Add flour; beat until smooth. Cover and refrigerate 1 hour. Lightly butter a 6-inch frypan. Pour 2 Tbs. of crêpe batter into pan; rotate pan quickly to spread evenly. Cook until lightly browned. Turn; brown lightly on second side and turn out. Keep warm.

Prepare filling. Cook contents of rice and seasoning packets according to package directions. Cook ground beef until crumbly; drain. Add cooked rice and mushrooms; mix well. Fill each crêpe with ⅓ cup rice mixture; roll up. Place on large heatproof platter or 13½ × 8½-inch baking dish.

Prepare sauce. Melt butter or margarine; stir in flour, then soup and milk. Cook until thickened, stirring constantly. Stir in remaining rice mixture. Pour over filled crêpes. Sprinkle with cheese. Bake at 350°F. oven until cheese is melted, 15 to 20 minutes. Makes 6 servings, 2 crêpes per serving.

Best Beef Bourguignon

True beef bourguignon from Holland House Wines.

½ lb. mushrooms, sliced
¼ cup butter
3 slices bacon, cut up
2 lbs. boneless beef, cut in 2-inch cubes
2 Tbs. flour
2 cloves garlic, crushed
1 Tbs. tomato paste
1¼ cups Holland House Red Cooking Wine

2 beef bouillon cubes
2 Tbs. sugar
¼ tsp. salt
¼ tsp. thyme
1 small bay leaf
1 peppercorn
½ lb. small white onions

In large pot, sauté mushrooms in butter; remove mushrooms and set aside. Fry bacon until crisp; remove and set aside. Add meat to drippings and brown well. Blend in flour. Add garlic, tomato paste, wine and seasonings. Cover and simmer for 2 hours, stirring occasionally. Add onions, mushrooms and bacon; simmer 1 hour longer. Add additional wine if liquid has evaporated. Garnish with cherry tomatoes and serve over rice if desired.

Best Ever Meat Loaf

In 1916 Campbell's published "Help for the Hostess," the first cookbook to use canned soup as an ingredient. This succulent meat loaf made its debut in the first edition and it's been going strong ever since. Here is the up-to-date version with four popular variations.

1 10¾-ounce can Campbell's Condensed Cream of Mushroom or Golden Mushroom Soup
2 lbs. ground beef
½ cup fine dry breadcrumbs
1 egg, slightly beaten
⅓ cup finely chopped onion
1 tsp. salt
⅓ cup water

Mix thoroughly ½ cup soup, beef, breadcrumbs, egg, onion, and salt. Shape *firmly* into loaf (8 × 4-inch); place in shallow baking pan. Bake at 375°F. for 1 hour, 15 minutes. In saucepan, blend remaining soup, water, and 2 to 3 Tbs. drippings. Heat; stir occasionally. Serve with loaf. Makes 6 to 8 servings.

Frosted Meat Loaf: Prepare loaf as above; bake for 1 hour. Frost loaf with 4 cups mashed potatoes; sprinkle with shredded Cheddar cheese. Bake 15 minutes more.

Swedish Meat Loaf: Add ½ tsp. nutmeg to loaf. Blend remaining soup with ⅓ cup sour cream; omit drippings and water. Serve over loaf; sprinkle with additional nutmeg. Garnish with thinly sliced cucumber.

Meat Loaf Wellington: Crescent Rolls (Refrigerated): Prepare loaf as above. Bake at 375°F. for 1 hour. Spoon off fat. Separate 1 package (8 ounces) refrigerated crescent dinner rolls; place crosswise over top and down sides of meat loaf, overlapping slightly. Bake 15 minutes more.

Patty Shells: Thaw 1 package (10 ounces) frozen patty shells. Prepare loaf as above. Bake at 375°F. for 30 minutes. Spoon off fat. Increase oven temperature to 400°F. On floured board, roll 5 patty shells into rectangle (12 × 8-inch); prick several times with fork. Cover top and sides of loaf with pastry. Decorate top with remaining patty shell, rolled and cut into fancy shapes. Bake 45 minutes more or until golden brown. Serve with sauce.

Souperburgers

Back in 1959 Campbell's test kitchens developed this "souper" easy hearty main dish. Good cooks around the country still write in for the recipe. The results never disappoint them.

1 lb. ground beef
½ cup chopped onion
1 can Campbell's Chicken Gumbo Soup

2 Tbs. catsup
1 Tbs. prepared mustard
6 buns, split and toasted

Brown beef and cook onion in skillet until tender (use shortening, if necessary); stir to separate meat. Add soup and seasonings. Heat; stir often. Serve on buns. Makes about 3 cups.

Hiram Walker's Supreme Brandy Burgers

These are supreme all right, just the best burgers I have ever devoured.

2 shallots (or scallions) finely chopped
4 Tbs. butter
1 lb. ground lean chuck
¼ lb. boiled ham, ground
4 Tbs. ice water
1 egg slightly beaten
Pinch of thyme
Freshly ground pepper

Flour
1 Tbs. oil
¼ cup beef consommé
¼ cup Hiram Walker Apricot Flavored Brandy
2 Tbs. butter
Parsley

Sauté the shallots, add the next 7 ingredients. Wet hands and shape into patties. Refrigerate for 1 hour. Dust patties with flour; sauté in oil and keep in warm oven. Add consommé, Apricot Brandy, and cook five minutes. Add butter and pour over patties. Sprinkle with parsley.

Old El Paso Guacamole

2 California avocados, peeled and barely mashed
⅓ cup onion, chopped
⅓ cup Old El Paso Chopped Green Chilies
⅔ cup tomato, chopped

2 Tbs. Old El Paso Taco Sauce
1 Tbs. lemon or lime juice
1¼ tsp. sugar
½ tsp. garlic powder

Prepare all ingredients. In a medium bowl, carefully mix all ingredients. Makes 2⅔ cups.

Double the recipe so you'll have plenty of this zesty dip for tortilla chips and chilled fresh vegetables. Will keep 2 to 3 days refrigerated.

Avocado Tostadas

"Next time you feel like having a little excitement, stay at home and enjoy it. Crunchy 'Old El Paso' Tostada Shells heaped with refried beans and ground beef; smothered with zesty California avocado guacamole and layers of shredded lettuce, olives and Cheddar. Top with even more cool, golden-green guacamole, and a dab of tangy sour cream. It's a feast for eight that you can make in minutes." The Avocado Advisory Board and Old El Paso Foods sent us these words about their Avocado Tostadas. All we can add is, bravo!

8 Old El Paso Tostada Shells	½ cup sliced black olives
1 can (16-ounces) Old El Paso Refried Beans	4 cups shredded lettuce
	1 cup grated Cheddar cheese
4 cups browned ground beef	½ cup sour cream
2¾ cups guacamole	Old El Paso Taco Sauce
	Season to taste

Prepare all ingredients. Heat tostada shells according to package directions. In separate skillets heat beans and browned meat. Assemble tostadas by spreading equal portions of beans on each shell. Next layer equal portions of meat and guacamole (reserving about ¾ cup guacamole to garnish tops of tostadas); add olives, lettuce and cheese. Top each with a large spoonful of guacamole and a dollop of sour cream. If desired, Old El Paso hot or mild Taco Sauce may be sprinkled over tostada. Makes 8 servings.

Tamale Pie

This is an "old love." Way back in depression days tamale pie made a great inexpensive supper. It still does. This version from Elam's Yellow Corn Meal box is extra good.

1½ cups cold water
1½ cups Elam's Stone
  Ground 100% Whole
  Yellow Corn Meal
1½ tsps. salt
  2 cups boiling water
  1 lb. ground beef chuck
  or round
  ½ cup chopped onion

2 Tbs. flour
1 tsp. chili powder
1 can (1 lb.) tomatoes
1 can (8 ounces) tomato
  sauce
1 can (8¾ ounces) whole
  kernel corn, drained (1
  cup)

Combine and mix cold water and corn meal. Add ½ tsp. salt to boiling water. Add corn-meal mixture, stirring constantly, bring to a boil. Partially cover pan; cook slowly 7 minutes, stirring often. Line bottom and sides of greased 2-quart casserole with cooked mush. Cook beef and onion in frypan until beef is brown and crumbly. Stir in flour, remaining 1 tsp. salt and chili powder. Add tomatoes, breaking them up into chunks with spoon. Stir in tomato sauce and corn. Spoon into mush-lined casserole. Bake in 350°F. oven until hot and bubbly, 40 to 45 minutes. Makes 6 servings.

Frito Chili Pie Casserole

Did you know the very first Fritos were made with an old converted potato ricer? Mrs. Daisy Dean Doolin (mother of Elmer Doolin, the founder of the Frito Company) was the cook and Elmer was the route salesman for the corn chips. Nobody seems to know just when some talented cook combined Fritos and chili in this casserole dish, but it's Fritos' most-asked-for recipe.

3 cups Fritos Brand Corn
  Chips
1 large onion, chopped

1 can (19 ounces) chili
1 cup grated American
  cheese

Place 2 cups of Fritos Brand Corn Chips in a baking dish. Arrange chopped onion and half of grated cheese on the corn chips. Pour chili over onion and cheese. Top with the remaining corn chips and grated cheese. Bake at 350° F. for 15 to 20 minutes. Makes 4 to 6 servings.

Enchiladas

Would a Texas girl like me put together a cookbook of famous recipes without one for enchiladas? Certainly not this one, so here is Kraft's classic version of this great dish.

1 lb. ground beef
1 16-ounce can tomatoes
1 6-ounce can tomato
  paste
½ cup water
½ cup chopped onion
1 Tbs. chili powder
1¼ tsps. salt

¼ tsp. pepper
1 8-ounce package
  tortillas
  Oil
2 cups (8 ounces)
  shredded Kraft sharp
  Cheddar cheese

Brown meat; drain. Add tomatoes, tomato paste, water, onion and seasonings; simmer 10 minutes. Fry tortillas in hot oil until softened; drain. Place rounded tablespoonful of meat sauce and cheese on each tortilla; roll up tightly. Place seam side down in 11¾ × 7½-inch baking dish; top with remaining sauce and cheese. Cover with aluminum foil; bake at 375°F. for 25 minutes. Makes 6 to 8 servings.

To make ahead: Prepare recipe as directed. Cover; refrigerate overnight. Bake at 375°F. for 50 minutes.

Hot Mexican Beef Salad

I'm sorry, I couldn't resist just one more South of the Border recipe. It's simply spectacular! Hot salad made with meat sauce, shredded lettuce and sharp Cheddar—festive and different for entertaining or family suppers.

1 lb. ground beef
¼ cup chopped onion
1 16-ounce can kidney beans, drained
½ cup Catalina French dressing
½ cup water
1 Tbs. chili powder
1 qt. shredded lettuce
½ cup sliced green onion
2 cups (8 ounces) shredded Kraft sharp Cheddar cheese

Brown meat; drain. Add onion; cook until tender. Stir in beans, dressing, water and chili powder; simmer 15 minutes. Combine lettuce and green onion. Add meat mixture and 1½ cups cheese; mix lightly. Top with remaining cheese. Makes 4 to 6 servings.

For variety, serve with toppings such as sour cream, sliced avocado, tortilla chips and sliced ripe olives.

Veal Parmigiana

Progresso Foods printed this Italian classic recipe on their Redi-Flavored Bread Crumbs package.

1 lb. veal cutlets
1 or 2 eggs, beaten Progresso Redi-Flavored Bread Crumbs
¼ cup Progresso Pure Olive Oil
1 8-ounce can Progresso Tomato Sauce
Progresso Grated Parmesan Cheese
Slices of Mozzarella cheese

Dip cutlets in beaten egg, then in bread crumbs, and fry in hot olive oil until golden-brown on both sides.

Place cutlets in a baking pan, pour tomato sauce over each, sprinkle with Parmesan cheese, and top each cutlet with slices of Mozzarella. Bake in a 375°F. oven for about 15 to 20 minutes, until Mozzarella has melted.

San Giorgio Marzetti

A Neapolitan-style recipe for a great casserole. Enjoy half tonight, freeze half for a work-free dinner whenever you're in the mood to dine *italiano*.

8 ounces San Giorgio Medium Egg Noodles
1 lb. lean ground beef
¾ cup finely chopped onion
½ tsp. salt
1 16-ounce jar San Giorgio Spaghetti Sauce with Mushrooms
½ cup green pepper slivers
½ cup thinly sliced celery
1 cup frozen peas
1 cup tomato juice
1 Tbs. Worcestershire sauce
½ tsp. crushed oregano
⅛ tsp. pepper
1 cup shredded Cheddar cheese
San Giorgio Grated Parmesan cheese

Prepare medium egg noodles as directed on package. Brown beef and onion in a heavy skillet until the pink disappears, breaking up the pieces as it cooks; pour off fat. Sprinkle the meat with salt. Add the remaining ingredients, except for cheeses. Simmer, covered for 10 minutes. Add the hot drained noodles and blend. Stir until hot; remove from heat. Blend in Cheddar cheese. Serve in a hot casserole, garnished with Parmesan cheese. Makes 8 (1 cup) servings.

Variation: If you desire, place half of the mixture in a freezer container, cover and freeze. Allow to defrost, sprinkle with buttered San Giorgio Seasoned Bread Crumbs and bake.

Lasagne Italiano

Authentic Italian lasagne—a Kraft "classic" from the mid-1950s.

1 lb. ground beef
½ cup chopped onion
1 6-ounce can tomato
   paste
1½ cups water
1 garlic clove, minced
2 tsps. salt
¾ tsp. oregano leaves
¼ tsp. pepper
8 ounces lasagne
   noodles, cooked,
   drained

1 lb. ricotta or cottage
   cheese
2 6-ounce packages Kraft
   Mozzarella cheese
   slices
½ cup grated Parmesan
   cheese

Brown meat; drain. Add onion; cook until tender. Stir in tomato paste, water and seasonings. Cover; simmer 30 minutes. In 11¾ × 7½-inch baking dish, layer half of noodles, meat sauce, ricotta cheese and Mozzarella cheese; repeat layers. Sprinkle with Parmesan cheese. Bake at 375°F. 30 minutes. Let stand 10 minutes before serving. Makes 6 to 8 servings.

Grand-Mott's Roast Pork

Was there anything ever as good as a roast of pork, crispy brown outside, done to a creamy turn inside? Yes, one that has been glazed with apple sauce, molasses and spices as in this recipe from the Mott's Apple Sauce jar.

4 to 6 lbs. pork loin roast
⅓ cup Mott's Apple Sauce
⅓ cup Grandma's
   Molasses

¼ tsp. ground ginger
1 clove garlic, crushed

Have meat retailer loosen chine (back) bone. Place roast

fat side up on rack in open roasting pan. Insert meat thermometer with bulb in thickest part not touching bone. Roast in 325°F. oven 2 to 2½ hours or until meat thermometer registers 170°F. In saucepan, combine apple sauce, molasses, ginger and garlic over medium heat. Brush pork with glaze every 10 minutes during last ½ hour of cooking. Serve pork with remaining apple sauce. Makes 8 to 10 servings.

Avocado With Chili Con Carne

If you have never tried chili with avocados you have never had one of the "specialties" of Southern California. The Avocado Advisory Board first published this super combination just a few years ago but its fame spread across the country in short order.

3 medium onions, coarsely chopped
4 cloves garlic
3 Tbs. bacon fat or butter
2 lbs. round of beef, diced
1 lb. lean pork, diced
⅓ cup chili powder
1 Tbs. flour
1 can (1 lb., 12 ounces) pear-shaped tomatoes

3 bay leaves
1 Tbs. *each:* salt, oregano, brown sugar, wine vinegar
2 cups pimiento-stuffed olives
4 avocados, halved and peeled

In large saucepan, cook onions and garlic in bacon fat until golden brown. Remove and reserve onions; discard garlic. Brown the meat in same pan over high heat. Stir in onions, chili powder and flour. Add tomatoes, bay leaves, salt, oregano, sugar and vinegar; bring to boil. Cover and simmer 2 hours, stirring occasionally. Discard bay leaves. Stir in olives; cook 30 minutes longer. Serve over avocado halves. Makes 8 servings.

Special Indoor Barbecued Spare Ribs With Sauce

From the Tabasco Sauce people in Creole Louisiana comes this classic red-hot barbecued ribs recipe. The sauce is equally good for barbecued chicken, and just try it over grilled hamburgers.

1 large onion, chopped	2 Tbs. honey
¼ cup Wesson Oil	2 tsps. Tabasco sauce
1 (6-ounce) can tomato paste	2 tsps. salt
½ cup water	1½ tsps. Liquid Smoke
1 beef bouillon cube	1 large clove garlic, minced
¼ cup Worcestershire sauce	1 tsp. dry mustard
¼ cup soy sauce	4 to 5 lb. pork spare ribs
¼ cup white vinegar	

In small saucepan, sauté onion in Wesson Oil until transparent. Add remaining ingredients except spare ribs. Mix well. Simmer 15 minutes. Pour over spare ribs in large glass baking dish; let stand 1 hour, turning occasionally. Arrange on shallow rack or broiler pan. Bake at 350° F. about 1½ to 2 hours. Turn ribs and baste with remaining barbecue sauce two or three times during baking. Cut in portions to serve. Makes 4 servings.

Cantonese Apricot Pork

The Apricot Advisory Board featured the recipe for this unusual Oriental dish in their advertising a decade ago; it's still an asked-for favorite. Perhaps it started today's popular trend toward using fruit in main-course recipes.

1½ lb. lean, boneless pork*
2 Tbs. salad oil
2 cups sliced celery
½ cup sliced scallions
2 large cloves garlic, minced
⅓ cup soy sauce
½ tsp. powdered ginger
1 8-ounce can water chestnuts, drained and sliced
1 30-ounce can apricot halves, drained
Salt, pepper
Rice

Slice pork into thin strips. Heat oil in wok; gradually add celery, scallions and garlic. Stir-fry over high heat (about 5 minutes) until tender but crisp; remove vegetables and set aside. Add pork to seasoned oil and stir-fry over high heat until lightly browned (about 10 minutes); mix in soy sauce and ginger. Reduce heat to medium; return vegetables to wok with water chestnuts; heat until hot, stirring constantly. Gently mix in apricots. Remove wok from heat immediately after mixing in apricots to prevent them from getting too soft. Season to taste with salt and pepper. Serve with rice. Makes 6 servings.

Lemony Ham Slice

A new idea from Oscar Mayer, so good they put it on their Oscar Mayer Jubilee Ham Slice package.

1 lemon
½ cup brown sugar
1 Tbs. prepared mustard
1 Oscar Mayer Ham Slice

Lemon Sauce: Grate peel of one lemon; cut lemon in half. Thinly slice one half; squeeze juice from other half. Combine peel, juice, brown sugar, mustard. Add lemon slices. Broil ham slice 4 inches from heat for 5 minutes;

* For a good money-saving dish use leftover pork.

turn and top with sauce. Broil 3 minutes until sauce bubbles. Makes 2 servings.

Quick Sweet and Sour Pork

Like Oriental food? You'll love this easy recipe from the label of Karo Corn Syrup.

2 Tbs. corn oil
1 lb. boneless pork, cut in 1-inch cubes
1 can (20 ounces) pineapple chunks in juice
½ cup Karo Light or Dark Corn Syrup
¼ cup cider vinegar

2 Tbs. catsup
2 Tbs. soy sauce
1 clove garlic, crushed
1 small pepper, cut in 1-inch squares
2 Tbs. corn starch
2 Tbs. water
Hot cooked rice or Chinese noodles

In large skillet heat corn oil over medium-high heat; add pork and brown on all sides. Add pineapple, corn syrup, vinegar, catsup, soy sauce and garlic. Bring to boil. Reduce heat; simmer uncovered, stirring occasionally, 10 minutes or until pork is tender. Add green pepper. Mix corn starch and water; stir into pork mixture. Stirring constantly, bring to boil over medium heat and boil 1 minute. Serve over rice or noodles. Serves 4.

Jambalaya

This 1898 Creole recipe came from the McIlhenny family who have been making Tabasco Sauce down on Avery Island in Louisiana for three-quarters of a century. The recipe first appeared in print back in the Thirties. Since then good cooks have made endless adaptations. Shrimp and chicken are favorite additions and the sausage is often omitted to suit today's taste for lighter meals.

½ lb. fresh pork
1 onion
1 clove garlic
½ lb. cured ham
6 small smoked pork sausages
2 Tbs. lard or butter
1 bay leaf
1 sprig parsley
1 sprig thyme or ¼ tsp. dried leaf thyme
1 whole clove
1½ quarts beef or chicken broth
½ tsp. Tabasco
¾ tsp. salt
1 cup uncooked rice

Cut pork (lean and fat) into cubes about ½-inch square. Chop onion and garlic very fine. Dice ham and cut sausage into pieces. Melt lard in a heavy iron pot or Dutch oven. Add onion, garlic, pork and ham; brown slowly, stirring frequently. Add sausage, bay leaf, parsley, thyme and clove; cook about 5 minutes. Add broth, Tabasco and salt; bring mixture to a boil. Add washed rice. Cover and simmer gently a half hour or longer until rice is tender. Stir often to mix well. Season to taste. Makes 4 to 6 servings.

Beans and Franks

Remember this? It's an old-time favorite combination. The recipe first appeared on Van Camp's Pork and Beans cans way back before World War II.

3 Tbs. chopped onion
2 Tbs. butter or margarine
1 can (1 lb., 15 ounces) Van Camp's Pork and Beans
6 wieners, sliced penny-style
⅓ cup brown sugar
1 tsp. prepared mustard
1 tsp. celery salt

Sauté onion in butter until tender. Combine onion with remaining ingredients in a 2-quart casserole. Bake, uncovered, at 350°F. for 40 minutes, stirring occasionally. Makes 6 servings.

Quiche Lorraine With Bacon

A lovely appetizer or a great luncheon or supper main dish. For cocktail party fare use this recipe from the Armour Bacon package for individual quiches, substituting 8 frozen tart shells for the pie shell.

1½ cups milk
 4 eggs, slightly beaten
 ½ tsp. salt
   Dash of cayenne
 2 cups (8 ounces) shredded Swiss cheese

2 Tbs. flour
½ lb. Armour Star Bacon, crisply cooked, crumbled
1 9-inch unbaked pastry shell

Heat oven to 350°F. Combine milk, eggs and seasonings; mix well. Toss cheese with flour; add cheese mixture and bacon to egg mixture. Pour into pastry shell. Bake at 350°F. 40 to 45 minutes. Makes 6 servings.

Kellogg's Crunchy Baked Chicken Variations

An easy delicious change from fried chicken.

Wash 3 lbs. frying chicken pieces. Pat dry. For any of the following variations, dip chicken in liquid mixture. Coat evenly with crumb mixture. Place in single layer, skin side up, in well-greased or foil-lined shallow baking pan. Drizzle with 3 Tbs. melted margarine, or butter if desired. Bake in oven at 350°F. about 1 hour or until chicken is tender. Do not cover pan or turn chicken while baking. Makes 6 servings.

Corn-Crisped Chicken: Dip in ½ cup evaporated milk. Coat with mixture of 1 cup Corn Flake Crumbs, 1 tsp. salt and ⅛ tsp. pepper.

California Crusty Chicken: Dip in mixture of ¼ cup melted margarine or butter, 3 Tbs. lemon juice and 1 tsp. grated lemon peel. Coat with mixture of 1¼ cups Corn Flake Crumbs, 1½ tsp. salt and ¼ tsp. pepper.

Baked Chicken Italiano: Dip in ½ cup Italian-style salad dressing. If desired, marinate chicken in dressing for at least 1 hour. Coat with 1¼ cups Corn Flake Crumbs.

Oven-Fried Chicken: Dip in mixture of 1 slightly beaten egg and 2 Tbs. milk. Coat with mixture of 1¼ cups Corn Flake Crumbs, 1½ tsps. salt and ¼ tsp. pepper.

Parmesan Crisped Chicken: Dip in mixture of 1 slightly beaten egg and 2 Tbs. milk. Coat with mixture of ¾ cup Corn Flake Crumbs, 1½ tsps. salt, ¼ tsp. pepper and ½ cup grated Parmesan cheese.

Zesty Crisped Chicken: Dip in mixture of 1 slightly beaten egg and ¼ cup soy sauce. Coat with 1¼ cups Corn Flake Crumbs.

Kellogg's Croutettes Roast Poultry Guide

Here's how to stuff and roast "le bird," be it chicken or turkey.

Wash poultry, drain and dry. Turn wing tips back. Spoon prepared Croutettes stuffing (see Stuffing Guide) into neck and body cavities. Fasten cavities by securing skin with skewers.

Place bird, breast side up, in roasting pan. Insert meat thermometer in inner thigh muscle. Brush skin with melted margarine or butter. Roast in oven at 325°F. until meat thermometer reaches 180°F. to 185°F.

To check stuffing temperature, remove thermometer from thigh and insert in body cavity. Thermometer should register 165°F. If meat thermometer is not used, allow about 25 minutes per pound, depending on size of bird. When drumstick moves up and down easily and leg joint gives readily, bird is done.

To bake extra stuffing, spoon into buttered baking dish, cover and bake at 350°F. about 30 minutes.

For Basic Stuffing, pour Croutettes croutons into large mixing bowl. Add melted margarine or butter while tossing gently. Stir lightly while adding hot water or stock. (Amount of water may be varied, depending on preference for a fluffy or moist stuffing.)

For Celery-Onion Stuffing, cook celery and onions in the melted margarine until tender before mixing with Croutettes croutons.

Croutettes Stuffing Guide

Poultry weight	3 – 5 lbs.	6 – 8 lbs.	9 – 11 lbs.	12 – 15 lbs.	16 – 19 lbs.	20 lbs. and over
Croutettes croutons (7-oz. pkg., 7 cups)	½ pkg.	1 pkg.	1½ pkgs.	2 pkgs.	2½ pkgs.	3 pkgs.
Melted margarine or butter	¼ – ⅓ cup	½ – ⅔ cup	¾ – 1 cup	1 – 1¼ cups	1¼ – 1½ cups	1½ – 2 cups
Hot water or stock	¾ cup	1½ cups	2¼ cups	3 cups	3¾ cups	4½ cups
Finely chopped celery	¼ cup	½ cup	1 cup	1 cup	1¼ cups	1½ cups
Chopped onions	2 Tbs.	¼ cup	½ cup	½ cup	⅔ cup	¾ cup

Chicken Oriental

The greatest recipes come from the most surprising people! This recipe from the jar of Mott's Apple Sauce is fabulously good. Try it and see.

2 to 3 lbs. chicken pieces

Marinade Ingredients:
1 cup Mott's Apple Sauce
½ cup soy sauce
1 clove garlic, minced
½ tsp. ground ginger
3 drops Tabasco

Combine marinade ingredients. Pour over meat. Refrigerate 8 to 12 hours. Drain meat and place on rack in baking pan. Bake covered for 1 hour at 350°F. Then uncover and baste with marinade; bake 15 minutes. Turn pieces, baste again, and bake for 15 more minutes. (Final "baking-and-basting" may be done on charcoal grill.) Makes 4 to 6 servings.

Chicken À L'Orange

Created by a famous French chef almost twenty years ago, this recipe appeared for years in Cointreau advertising; it's an especially pretty dish for a dinner party.

2 broiler-size (2- to 2½-lb.) chickens, quartered
2 Tbs. butter
½ tsp. salt
¼ tsp. pepper
¼ tsp. paprika
¼ tsp. dried tarragon
½ cup minced green onion
1 clove garlic, peeled and minced
½ cup finely chopped celery
4 more Tbs. butter
¼ cup Cointreau
2 Tbs. lemon juice
2 cups chicken stock or broth
¼ cup tomato paste
Minced parsley for garnish

Preheat oven to 375°F. Arrange quartered chicken pieces in a long shallow baking dish. Bake in preheated oven for 30 minutes, turning pieces twice during cooking. In a small skillet melt butter, stir in salt, pepper, paprika and tarragon; pour evenly over chicken pieces. Continue to bake for about 15 minutes, until chicken is tender and browned. While chicken bakes prepare sauce; sauté onion, garlic and celery in butter until soft. Add remaining ingredients; stir until blended; bring to boil; lower heat and let simmer very gently about 30 minutes or until thick and smooth. Arrange chicken pieces on serving platter. Pour sauce over and sprinkle with parsley. Makes 8 servings.

Broiled Chicken Italiano

This is so easy and so good you'll wonder why no one thought of it before. The Wish-Bone Salad Dressing people did, back in 1972 when it appeared on their Italian Dressing label.

2½- to 3-lb. chicken, cut into
    serving pieces
    Salt
½ cup Wish-Bone Italian
    Dressing

Place chicken on broiler rack, sprinkle with salt and brush with Wish-Bone Italian Dressing. Broil about 45 minutes, basting with remaining dressing and turning chicken frequently. Makes about 4 servings.

Tangy Chicken

The Heinz Company has been printing this extra-easy chicken recipe on their 57 Sauce bottles for years. It's such a favorite customers probably wouldn't let them take it off.

2 to 2½ lbs. broiler-fryer pieces
2 Tbs. butter or margarine

½ cup Heinz 57 Sauce
½ cup water

Brown chicken in skillet in butter. Combine 57 Sauce and water; pour over chicken. Cover; simmer, basting occasionally, 30 to 40 minutes or until chicken is tender. Remove cover last 10 minutes of cooking. Skim excess fat from sauce before serving. Spoon sauce over chicken. Makes 4 servings (about ¾ cup sauce).

Baked Chicken That Makes Its Own Gravy

In 1964 the Carnation Evaporated Milk label featured this savory recipe for chicken, and it's been an asked-for special ever since. Chicken and gravy fans love it. Add hot cooked rice and a tomato salad for a true Deep-South supper.

3 to 3½ lbs. frying chicken pieces
¼ cup flour
¼ cup melted butter
⅔ cup undiluted Carnation Evaporated Milk
1 can (10¾ ounces) condensed cream of mushroom soup

1 cup (4 ounces) grated process American cheese
½ tsp. salt
⅛ tsp. pepper
2 cups (1-lb. can) drained whole onions
¼ lb. sliced mushrooms
Dash paprika

Coat chicken with flour. Arrange chicken in single layer with skin down in melted butter in 13 × 9 × 2-inch baking dish. Bake uncovered in 425°F. oven for 30 minutes. Turn chicken, bake until brown, 15 to 20 minutes longer, until tender. Remove from oven and reduce temperature to 325°F. Pour off excess fat. Combine Carnation, soup, cheese, salt and pepper. Add onions and mushrooms to chicken. Pour Carnation mixture over chicken. Sprinkle with paprika. Cover dish with foil. Return to oven for 15 to 20 minutes. Serves 6.

Chicken With Lime

Every year the Delmarva Chicken Association (*Delaware/Maryland/Virginia*,) sponsors a chicken cooking contest. For one of the "best of the best" try this 1977 winning recipe created by Mrs. Sally B. Lilley of Chevy Chase, Maryland.

1 broiler-fryer chicken, cut in parts	½ tsp. ground cumin
1 tsp. salt	½ tsp. ground coriander seed
¼ tsp. black pepper	¼ tsp. crushed red pepper
¼ cup corn oil	¼ tsp. turmeric
1 Tbs. minced onion	2 Tbs. soy sauce
1 clove garlic, minced	2 limes, quartered

Sprinkle chicken with salt and black pepper. Heat corn oil in large fry pan over medium heat. Add chicken and brown on all sides. Push chicken to side of pan. Add onion and garlic; sauté until golden. Add cumin, coriander, red pepper and turmeric. Stir around to distribute. Add soy sauce. Reduce heat and cook slowly, covered, stirring frequently about 20 minutes or until fork can be inserted in chicken with ease. Serve over rice. Squeeze 1 lime on chicken before serving, section remaining lime to squeeze on chicken while eating. Makes 4 servings.

Progresso's Chicken Cacciatore

A virtual Italian opera of flavors. Serve it with piping-hot just-cooked spaghetti and freshly grated Parmesan cheese.

2½- to 3-lb. spring chicken, cut into pieces
¼ cup Progresso Pure Olive Oil
1 medium onion, chopped
1 clove garlic, minced
1 tsp. Progresso Basil
1 Tbs. parsley
¼ cup Sherry, Marsala or white wine
Salt and pepper
1 can (17-ounce) Progresso Peeled Tomatoes, cut up (or ½ 35-ounce can)

Brown chicken pieces in hot olive oil until lightly colored; add onion, garlic, basil and parsley and brown along with chicken until chicken is golden-brown and vegetables are soft and slightly colored. Wet with wine and allow to evaporate. Season with salt and pepper to taste. Add tomatoes and their juices. Cover and simmer for about 20 to 30 minutes or until chicken is tender and sauce has thickened a little.

Easy Chicken Tetrazzini

Ehlers Gravy Mix for Chicken makes short work of a very special supper dish from this recipe printed on the Ehlers envelope for the past five years. Madame Tetrazzini, who inspired the original dish, would have approved.

1 8-ounce package spaghetti
1 envelope Ehlers Gravy Mix for Chicken
1¼ cups milk
¼ cup cooking sherry
2 cups cooked, cubed chicken
1 4-ounce can sliced mushrooms, drained
2 Tbs. grated Parmesan cheese

Preheat oven to 350°F. Prepare spaghetti as label directs; drain. Place spaghetti in a greased 8-inch-square baking dish. Mix together remaining ingredients, except cheese. Pour mixture over spaghetti. Sprinkle with cheese. Bake 45 minutes, until bubbly. Let stand 5 minutes before serving. Makes 4 servings.

Chicken Macaroni Triumph

An elegant party dish, flavored with white wine. Easy and quick, it's from Mueller's Sea Shell Macaroni package.

3 whole chicken breasts, boned, skin removed
3 slices boiled ham, cut in half
3 slices American cheese, cut in half
2 Tbs. butter or margarine
1 (10¾ ounce) can condensed cream of mushroom soup
½ cup dry white wine
¼ cup milk or light cream
Salt and pepper
8 ounces (3½ to 4 cups) Mueller's Sea Shell Macaroni
1 9-ounce package frozen cut green beans, cooked

Cut chicken breasts in half; pound with flat side of knife. On each piece of chicken place a piece of ham and cheese. Roll, tucking cheese in; fasten with toothpicks. Brown rolls in butter in skillet; remove toothpicks; place in 11 × 8 × 2-inch baking dish. Blend soup, wine and milk into drippings; season to taste with salt and pepper; pour over chicken. Bake at 350°F. about 45 minutes or until tender. Meanwhile, cook macaroni as directed on package; drain. In large serving dish, combine green beans and macaroni; stir in sauce from chicken; arrange chicken rolls on top. Makes 4 to 6 servings.

Avocado With Curried Chicken

This heavenly idea was introduced by the Avocado Advisory Board a dozen years ago. It's a gourmet dish, perfect for a festive lunch or supper party, and it probably started today's popular trend for serving hot avocado main dishes.

¼ cup butter (½ stick)
½ cup chopped pared apple
¼ cup chopped onion
1 clove garlic, crushed
1 Tbs. curry powder
¼ cup flour
1 cup light cream
1 cup chicken bouillon

1 tsp. salt
⅛ tsp. pepper
2 cups cut-up, cooked chicken
3 or 4 avocados, halved and peeled
3 to 4 cups cooked rice
Condiments, given below

In saucepan, sauté apple, onion, garlic and curry powder in butter until onion is crisp-tender. Stir in flour. Gradually add cream and bouillon; cook and stir until sauce boils 1 minute. Add salt, pepper and chicken. Cook over low heat 10 minutes. Arrange avocado halves on rice in heat-proof serving dish. Heat in 350°F. (moderate) oven about 5 minutes. Spoon curried chicken over avocado halves. Serve with Indian or Euphrates bread and a choice of these condiments: chopped egg, crumbled bacon, sweet mixed pickles, coconut, raisins, chutney, Bombay duck, preserved ginger, chopped peanuts. Makes 6 servings.

Baked Chicken Salad

Here's a really different chicken recipe people have asked for time and time again.

2 Tbs. corn oil margarine
1 cup thinly sliced celery
½ cup chopped onion
½ cup Hellmann's Real Mayonnaise or Best Foods Real Mayonnaise
½ cup dairy sour cream
1 Tbs. lemon juice
½ tsp. salt

⅛ tsp. pepper
2 cups cubed cooked chicken
½ cup slivered almonds, toasted
1 can (6 ounces) sliced mushrooms, drained
¼ cup crushed potato chips

In large skillet melt margarine over medium heat. Add celery and onion; cook about 4 minutes or until tender. Remove from heat. Stir in next 5 ingredients until well blended. Add chicken, almonds and mushrooms; toss to coat well. Spoon into 1½-quart casserole. Sprinkle with potato chips. Bake in 325°F. oven 25 to 30 minutes or until hot. Makes 4 to 6 servings.

Microwave Directions: In 1½-quart microproof casserole microwave margarine with full power until melted. Stir in celery and onion; microwave 3 minutes. Stir in next 5 ingredients. Add chicken, almonds and mushrooms; toss to coat well. Microwave 5 minutes or until hot, stirring once and sprinkling with potato chips after 3 minutes.

Tyson's Food's Kintail Cornish Game Hens

The original recipe bowed in 1970 in a Tyson ad; it's a festive way to serve these versatile birds and an especially pretty dinner-party mainstay. Count on one whole bird per guest. There won't be any leftovers!

2 Tyson brand Cornish Hens, thawed

1 cup cooked wild rice (or mixture wild and long grain) with some chopped apple pieces and chopped pecans added

3 Tbs. butter or margarine

8 Tbs. orange marmalade

2 Tbs. lemon juice

¼ cup brandy

Salt cavity and stuff game hens with rice, apple, pecan mixture. Place hens on foil in pan. Over medium heat, melt butter. Add orange marmalade, lemon juice and brandy. Stir until heated. Brush some of marmalade mixture over hens, coating them well. Cover hens with foil. Bake in a preheated 350°F. oven for 30 minutes. Uncover and baste frequently with pan drippings and more marmalade mixture, adding more brandy if desired, for one hour more. Makes 2 servings.

Tyson's Cornish Hens Steamed in Foil

Tyson Foods advertised their Cornish hens with this easy recipe just a few years ago, but it became so popular it's termed a classic.

4 Tyson brand Cornish Hens, thawed

For each Cornish Hen:

1 square of foil, 16 inches at least

¼ tsp. sage or thyme

1 sprig parsley

½ tsp. salt 1 to 2 tsp. butter
    Few grindings pepper

Preheat oven to 350°F. Season each hen with salt, pepper, sage or thyme. Place on foil, lay a sprig of parsley on top of hen and wrap securely in foil. Place hens on baking sheet or in baking pan. Place in oven for 1 hour. Remove hens and raise heat to 425°F. Carefully open foil (watch out for escaping steam) to expose hens. Brush with butter and return to oven to brown for 5 to 10 minutes. Serve hens with juices accumulated in foil. Makes 4 servings.

Crispy Fried Fish

"Even people who aren't enthusiastic about fish love this recipe. We've made it on lots of seaside "cookouts" over fires built in the sand with fish caught minutes before," says the director of the R. T. French Company's test kitchen. This unusual recipe appeared in French's advertising in 1972.

2 eggs
¼ cup French's Prepared
    Mustard
1 tsp. French's Parsley
    Flakes
½ tsp. French's Seafood
    Seasoning

1½ lbs. fish fillets
French's Big Tate
Mashed Potato Flakes
Oil or melted
shortening

Beat together eggs, mustard, parsley, and seafood seasoning. Dip fish in the mustard mixture; roll in potato flakes. Fry in hot oil or shortening 3 to 4 minutes on each side or until fish flakes easily and is golden brown. Makes 4 servings.

TWO OUTSTANDING SAUCES FOR FISH FROM SUNKIST LEMONS

Shakespeare wrote:
". . . the sauce
to meat is ceremony:
Meeting were bare without it."

Which is very true, and if you would transform simple broiled fish, whip up one of these sauces from the Sunkist Lemon people's advertising—they are indeed "repeat specials."

Lemon Mustard Sauce

2 Tbs. butter or margarine
2 Tbs. flour
½ tsp. salt
⅛ tsp. pepper
1 cup hot water

1 tsp. prepared mustard
Grated peel and juice of
½ fresh Sunkist Lemon
½ cup mayonnaise or
salad dressing

In saucepan, melt butter. Remove from heat; stir in flour, salt and pepper. Gradually blend in water and mustard. Cook over medium heat, stirring until thickened. Add lemon peel and juice. Remove from heat; blend in mayonnaise. Makes about 1⅓ cups.

Lemon Tartar Sauce

½ cup mayonnaise or
  salad dressing
2 Tbs. finely chopped dill
  pickle
2 Tbs. finely chopped
  green onion

1 Tbs. chopped canned
  pimiento, optional
1 tsp. fresh grated Sunkist
  Lemon peel
2 tsps. fresh squeezed
  lemon juice

In small bowl, combine all ingredients. Makes about ¾
cup.

Clam Crunch

**I am fascinated by this recipe and the story behind it.
Ralston Purina tells me it was "one of the winners in our
Chex Create-A-Recipe Contest several years ago. It was
sent in by a ninety-one-year-old Connecticut woman."**

¼ cup all-purpose flour
½ tsp. baking powder
¼ tsp. salt
⅛ tsp. black pepper
1 Tbs. snipped parsley
1 (6½-ounce) can minced
  clams, drained (reserve
  liquid)

1 egg, beaten
2 cups Rice Chex cereal
  Cooking oil
  Sour cream, optional

In medium bowl combine flour, baking powder, salt,
pepper and parsley. Slowly stir in clam liquid until
smooth. Add egg and clams. Mix well. Stir in Rice Chex
to coat. Let stand 10 minutes. Stir to combine. Heat oil
(⅛-inch deep) in skillet. Drop 1 heaping tablespoon clam
mixture into hot oil. Pat with spoon to form 3-inch patty.
Repeat to form 8 patties. Brown over medium heat.
Turn. Brown. Drain on absorbent paper. Serve immediately. Top with sour cream if desired. Makes 4 servings.

Scrumptious Shrimp Suprême

This title from Wish Bone Salad Dressing may sound a bit fancy but wait until you taste it! Serve with a medley of rice, peas and parsley for a perfect shore-side dinner.

1 (8-ounce) bottle Wish-
Bone Italian Dressing
1 cup chili sauce
2 Tbs. corn syrup

2 lbs. large shrimp, shelled
and cleaned
4 lemons, cut into wedges

In large bowl, blend Wish-Bone Italian Dressing with chili sauce and corn syrup; add shrimp. Cover and marinate in refrigerator 2 hours, turning occasionally. On skewers, alternately thread shrimp and lemons. Grill or broil, turning and basting frequently with remaining marinade, 15 minutes or until shrimp is done. Makes about 6 servings.

Crabby Rice Enchiladas

A truly unusual and delicious idea for a party, lunch or supper from Uncle Ben's Rice.

1 cup Uncle Ben's
Converted Brand Rice
1 or 2 6-ounce packages
frozen crabmeat,
thawed and diced
¼ cup chopped green
onion
½ lb. Monterey Jack
cheese, shredded

1 10-ounce can enchilada
sauce
⅓ cup cooking oil
16 corn tortillas
1 cup dairy sour cream
(more if desired)
Pitted ripe olives,
quartered, for garnish—
optional

Cook rice according to package directions. Stir crabmeat, onion, 1 cup cheese and 3 Tbs. enchilada sauce into cooked rice. Heat oil in small skillet. Heat tortillas, one at a time, until soft. Drain on paper toweling. Spread each tortilla down center with about ¼ cup rice mixture. Roll up. Arrange in 13½ × 8½-inch baking dish. Pour remaining enchilada sauce over tortillas. Cover with aluminum foil, crimping it tightly to edges of dish. Bake at 350°F. for 25 minutes. Uncover. Sprinkle with remaining cheese. Return to oven until thoroughly heated and cheese melts, 5 to 10 minutes. Top with sour cream; garnish with olives if desired. Makes 8 servings.

Southern Shrimp and Dumplings

A great way to make a small amount of shrimp into a delicious dinner for four, from the Mueller's Dumpling Macaroni package.

2 Tbs. butter or margarine
½ cup thinly sliced onion
½ cup thinly sliced green pepper
1 clove garlic, mashed
1 can (1 pound) tomatoes
2 tsps. salt
⅛ tsp. pepper
Dash cayenne
2 bay leaves
8 ounces cooked shrimp
6 ounces (3 cups) Mueller's Dumpling Macaroni

Melt butter in skillet; add onion, green pepper and garlic; cook until crisp-tender but not brown. Stir in tomatoes and seasonings; cover and simmer about 10 minutes. Add shrimp; heat a few minutes; remove bay leaves. Meanwhile, cook macaroni as directed on package; drain. Serve shrimp mixture over macaroni. Makes 4 servings.

Seven Seas Casserole

Apparently this speedy, delicious casserole is a winning combination, a flavorful mix of rice, tuna, peas and cheese, for the recipe first appeared on the Minute Rice box in 1957.

1⅓ cups water
1 (10¾-ounce) can condensed cream of mushroom or celery soup
¼ cup finely chopped onion, optional
1 tsp. lemon juice, optional
¼ tsp. salt
Dash of pepper

1⅓ cups Minute Rice
1 (10-ounce) package Birds Eye 5 Minute Sweet Green Peas, partially thawed
1 (7-ounce) can tuna, drained and flaked
½ cup grated Cheddar cheese
Paprika

Combine water, soup, onion, lemon juice, salt and pepper in a saucepan. Bring to a boil, stirring occasionally, over medium heat. Pour about half of soup mixture into a greased 1½-quart casserole. Then, in separate layers, add rice, peas and tuna. Add remaining soup mixture. Sprinkle with cheese and paprika. Cover and bake at 375°F. for 10 minutes. Stir; then cover and continue baking for 10 to 15 minutes longer. Makes about 5½ cups or 4 servings.

Perfect Tuna Casserole

How many ovens in the United States and around the world have baked this famous casserole?

1 10¾-ounce can Campbell's Condensed Cream of Celery or Mushroom Soup

¼ cup milk
2 hard-cooked eggs, sliced
1 cup cooked peas

1 can tuna (about 7 ounces), drained and flaked

½ cup slightly crumbled potato chips

In 1-quart casserole, blend soup and milk; stir in tuna, eggs and peas. Bake at 350°F. for 25 minutes or until hot; stir. Top with chips; bake 5 minutes more. Makes about 4 cups.

Pacific Salmon Loaf

The cooks at Kraft tell us this salmon, cucumber and dill combination is a favorite with their television viewers.

1 16-ounce can salmon, drained, flaked
½ cup dry bread crumbs
½ cup Kraft Real Mayonnaise
½ cup chopped onion

¼ cup chopped celery
¼ cup chopped green pepper
1 egg, beaten
1 tsp. salt
Cucumber Sauce

Combine ingredients except Cucumber Sauce; mix lightly. Shape into loaf in shallow baking dish. Bake at 350°F. for 40 minutes. Serve with:

Cucumber Sauce

½ cup Kraft Real Mayonnaise
½ cup dairy sour cream
½ cup finely chopped cucumber

2 Tbs. chopped onion
½ tsp. dill weed

Combine ingredients; mix well. Makes 6 to 8 servings.

3.
Side Dishes: Vegetables, Potatoes, Beans, Pasta and Such

Do you know that for years I regarded fried tomatoes as in a league with spun sugar? Both were impossible for me to master and while the need was never pressing to concoct those spun-sugar fairy-tale desserts I had seen only in illustrations, last summer's bountiful harvest of tomatoes demanded I do something with all those red beauties. I determined to master fried tomatoes. After several soggy failures I had just about given up when I found a batch of recipes from the Pet Milk Company. Among them, oh happy day, was a recipe for fried tomatoes—and, wonder of wonders, it worked! These were the crispy-surfaced, luscious fried tomatoes of my dreams. I can tell you, I fried tomatoes just about every day until the first frost ended my tomato orgy. I even served them for Sunday breakfast, they were that good. Now I don't say you can get the same results with "store-bought" tomatoes but you can glorify even a lesser tomato with the Pet recipe. If ever I doubted that those home economists who test all the recipes for our food companies really know their business, I don't now. Their recipes *work!* That may sound very simple, but I've been cooking a long time and many a respected recipe doesn't work. I guess that's why I have enjoyed putting this book together. Every recipe I've tried has been a resounding success, and when you add the imagination and creativity that have gone into each one to its sure-fire accuracy—well now, that's a recipe.

Good side dishes are great budget stretchers, you know. Try Creamy Seasoned Noodles the next time you serve pot roast, or Corn 'n Pepper Fritters with oven-fried chicken. Campbell's Green Bean Bake is a great casserole to complement a thrifty meat loaf, and if you would add an elegant touch to a dinner party, try the easy Blender Hollandaise Sauce over steamed broccoli or asparagus.

I hope you will try all the side dishes here, simple or not so simple. You'll find they add great enjoyment and variety to every meal and some, such as Cheese-Stuffed Eggplant, are meals in themselves. Good eating, every one of them!

"PET" VEGETABLES

In 1932 the Pet Milk Company published their "Gold Cookbook." In those days, deep in the Great Depression, every cook was economy-minded, and recipes had to be thrifty as well as good. Here, from that cookbook of almost fifty years ago, are four all-time favorite ways with vegetables, as economical as they are great-tasting.

Fried Tomatoes (Batter Dipped Tomatoes)

4 medium tomatoes, half
  ripe
½ cup all-purpose flour
2½ tsps. salt
2½ tsps. sugar

¼ tsp. pepper
¾ cup Pet Evaporated
  Milk
Oil for frying

Wash tomatoes, but do not peel. Cut into ¾-inch slices. Place on paper towels to drain. Combine flour, salt, sugar and pepper. Dust tomatoes in flour mixture on both sides. Add evaporated milk to remaining flour mixture to make a thick batter. Dip floured tomatoes in batter. Fry in hot oil ½-inch deep until golden brown on both sides. Makes 6 servings.

Creamed Spinach

Evaporated milk gives a mild flavor.

    1 lb. fresh spinach
    2 Tbs. all-purpose flour
    ½ cup Pet Evaporated Milk
    ¼ tsp. salt
       Few grains pepper

Wash spinach thoroughly. Shake water out of leaves.
Tear leaves into bite-size pieces. Place in saucepan.
Cover. Cook over low heat for 8 minutes or until tender.
The water that clings to the leaves is enough to cook the
spinach. Drain. Sprinkle flour over spinach. Stir to evenly
coat leaves. Add evaporated milk, salt and pepper.
Heat until sauce thickens. Makes 4 servings, ¼ cup
each.

Carrots in Onion Sauce

    ¼ cup finely chopped
       onion
    2 Tbs. oil
    2 cups diced carrots,
       cooked and drained
    ⅓ cup Pet Evaporated Milk
    ¼ tsp. salt
       Few grains pepper

Cook onion in hot oil over medium heat until limp. Stir
in carrots, evaporate milk, salt, and pepper. Cook over
low heat stirring gently until sauce coats the carrots and
is slightly thickened. Serve hot. Makes 4 servings, ½ cup
each.

Corn Pudding

2 cans (8¾ ounces each)
  corn
2 eggs, slightly beaten
¾ cup Pet Evaporated Milk

2 Tbs. margarine or
  butter, melted
1 tsp. salt
⅛ tsp. pepper

Mix well all ingredients. Pour into a greased 1½-quart baking dish. Bake at 350°F. for 45 minutes, until firm. Makes 6 servings, ½ cup each.

The Planters Peanut Oil cooks created these vegetable recipes. Each one is Italian-inspired. They will add great taste and good eating to any lunch, supper or dinner.

Broccoli Sauté

2 lbs. fresh broccoli
½ cup water
¼ cup Planters Peanut Oil

2 cloves garlic, minced
1 tsp. salt
⅛ tsp. pepper

Wash broccoli. Split ends of large stalks lengthwise into halves or quarters, depending on size. Place in large skillet. Sprinkle with water, Planters Peanut Oil, garlic, salt and pepper. Cover tightly; cook over very low heat 20 to 30 minutes, or until stalks are tender. Turn broccoli several times during cooking. Makes 4 servings.

Baked Eggplant Napoli

½ cup chopped onion
2 Tbs. Planters Peanut Oil
1 can (10½ ounces) tomato purée
⅔ cup water
1½ tsps. salt

1 tsp. oregano leaves
Dash pepper
1 medium eggplant, peeled and thinly sliced
2 cups grated sharp Cheddar cheese

In a skillet sauté chopped onions in Planters Peanut Oil. Add tomato purée, water, salt, oregano and pepper. Bring to a boil and simmer for 15 minutes.

In a greased 2-quart baking dish alternate layers of sliced eggplant, tomato sauce and 1 cup grated cheese, starting with layer of eggplant and ending with layer of tomato sauce.

Bake in moderate oven (350°F.) for 1 hour. A few minutes before removing from oven, sprinkle remaining 1 cup grated cheese over top and continue heating until cheese melts. Makes 6 to 8 servings.

Zucchini Parmesan

¼ cup Planters Peanut Oil
8 medium zucchini, thinly sliced
⅔ cup coarsely chopped onion
2 Tbs. chopped parsley
1 large clove garlic, crushed or minced

1 Tbs. salt
¼ tsp. pepper
¼ tsp. oregano leaves
¼ tsp. rosemary leaves
4 cups peeled chopped tomatoes
½ cup grated Parmesan cheese

Heat Planters Peanut Oil in large skillet. Add zucchini, onion, parsley, garlic, salt, pepper, oregano and rosemary. Sauté mixture over medium heat, stirring often, until zucchini is tender, about 20 minutes. Toss in tomatoes and continue to sauté until tomatoes are thoroughly heated, about 5 minutes. Turn mixture into a serving dish; sprinkle with Parmesan cheese. Makes 8 to 10 servings.

Orange-Glazed Beets

This recipe has been around since the Twenties, and each time Stokely takes it off their Finest Cut Beets label, the outcry from customers makes them put it right back on again.

1 can (1 lb.) Stokely's Finest Cut Beets	2 tsps. flour
1 Tbs. butter or margarine	2 Tbs. brown sugar
	½ cup orange juice

Heat beets in their own liquid. In small saucepan, melt butter. Remove from heat; add flour, brown sugar and orange juice. Return to heat, stirring constantly until thickened. Drain beets; add sauce to beets. Makes 4 to 5 servings.

Orange Carrots

Remember Orange-Glazed Carrots? I'll bet your mother made them from this recipe first printed in a Sunkist advertisement a generation ago.

1 lb. carrots	2 Tbs. margarine or butter
¾ cup water	2 to 3 Tbs. of your favorite
¾ tsp. salt	syrup (cane, molasses,
½ tsp. fresh grated orange peel	honey, pancake or brown sugar)
1 Sunkist orange	

Wash and peel, scrub or scrape carrots. Slice crosswise into rounds or lengthwise into sticks. Bring water and salt to a boil in saucepan. Add carrots and cover pan. Cook over medium heat for 10 to 20 minutes, until tender. Drain well. Meanwhile grate ½ tsp. peel from orange. Peel orange and cut into bite-size pieces. Add orange pieces and peel, margarine and syrup to drained carrots. Place over low heat and stir gently until margarine is melted and oranges are heated. Serve at once. Makes 6 servings.

Note: For different flavor, leave out the syrup and add 1 to 2 Tbs. finely chopped green onions or chives.

Green Bean Bake

In the Sixties Campbell's kitchens introduced this all-time favorite Green Bean Casserole; it's an inspired combination of creamy sauce, green beans and crispy onion rings.

1 10¾-ounce can
  Campbell's Condensed
  Cream of Mushroom
  Soup
½ cup milk
1 tsp. soy sauce
  Dash of pepper

2 packages (9 ounces
  each) frozen green
  beans, cooked and
  drained
1 can (3½ ounces) French
  fried onions

In 1½-quart casserole, stir soup, milk, soy, and pepper until smooth; mix in green beans and ½ can onions. Bake at 350°F. for 25 minutes; stir. Top with remaining onions. Bake 5 minutes more. Makes about 4 cups.

Blender Hollandaise Sauce

Sunkist introduced this fool-proof Hollandaise Sauce several years ago; it's guaranteed not to curdle and it's a sure-fire way to transform steamed broccoli, asparagus or grilled tomatoes into an epicurean dish.

½ cup butter or margarine
  (1 stick)
4 egg yolks

2–3 Tbs. fresh squeezed
  lemon juice
¼ tsp. salt
Dash of pepper

Heat butter or margarine until bubbly. Meanwhile, place egg yolks, fresh lemon juice, salt and pepper in electric blender. Turn blender on and off quickly. Then turn to high speed and slowly add bubbly butter in a very thin but steady stream. Serve immediately over broccoli, asparagus, or grilled tomatoes. Also good on fish or for Eggs Benedict. Makes about 1 cup.

Corn 'N' Pepper Fritters

Planters Peanut Oil ran this recipe in an ad a few seasons back and I tried it then. I had to include it here for you because it's one of the best of its kind.

1 egg
½ cup milk
1 can (12 ounces) golden
  whole kernel corn with
  sweet peppers,
  undrained
1 Tbs. Planters Peanut Oil

1½ cups unsifted flour
1 Tbs. baking powder
1 tsp. salt
Dash pepper
Planters Peanut Oil

Beat egg in large bowl. Stir in milk, corn and 1 Tbs. Planters Peanut Oil. Add and beat in flour, baking powder, salt and pepper.

Drop by tablespoonfuls into deep or shallow hot

(375°F.) Planters Peanut Oil. Fry until golden brown, 2 to 3 minutes on each side. Drain on paper towels. Serve hot. If desired, serve with syrup. Makes about 24 fritters.

Note: I like them best fried in deep oil. I think you will too.

Sweet Sour Shellie Beans

Do you know what Shellie Beans are? I didn't until I found this recipe on the Stokely Shellie Bean can. It's a great dish to serve with pork.

2 strips bacon
⅓ cup onion, finely diced
1 1-lb. can Stokely's Finest Shellie Beans
1 Tbs. sugar
⅛ tsp. salt
Few grains pepper
2 Tbs. white distilled vinegar

Cut bacon in ½-inch pieces. Brown lightly with diced onion. Add liquid drained from Shellie Beans. Cook down to about ½ cupful. Add remaining ingredients and Shellie Beans. Heat and serve. Makes 4 servings.

Apple Kraut Bavarian

What a lovely supper dish, dreamed up for Stokely's Sauerkraut label a few years ago.

1 10-ounce package brown and serve sausage links
1 1-lb. can Stokely's Finest Bavarian Style Sauerkraut, drained
1 1 lb., 1-ounce can Stokely's Finest Applesauce

In large skillet, brown sausage links. Add remaining ingredients to skillet and heat to serving temperature. Delicious with mashed potatoes. Makes 4 servings.

Southern Cheese-Stuffed Eggplant

The lovely thing about this delicious recipe from Armour's Miss Wisconsin Cheddar Cheese package is that it can serve nicely as an extra good luncheon or supper main dish. It's quick and easy too!

2 eggplants, cut in half lengthwise
½ cup chopped onion
½ cup chopped green pepper
½ cup butter or margarine
2 tomatoes, peeled, chopped
1 tsp. salt
½ tsp. pepper
1 8-ounce package Miss Wisconsin Medium Sharp Cheddar Cheese, shredded
1½ cups bread crumbs

Heat oven to 350°F. Scoop out interior of eggplants, leaving ¼-inch shell. Cube scooped-out interior; reserve. In large fry pan, cook onion and green pepper in ¼ cup butter or margarine on medium-low heat 5 minutes. Add tomatoes, salt, pepper and reserved cubed eggplant; cook 5 minutes. Drain liquid from vegetables. Stir in cheese and ½ cup bread crumbs. Spoon mixture into eggplant shells; place in greased 13 × 9-inch baking dish. Toss remaining bread crumbs with ¼ cup melted butter or margarine; sprinkle on top of stuffed eggplants. Bake at 350°F. for 30 minutes. Makes 8 servings.

Spaghetti With Zucchini Sauce

Vegetables and pasta that can solo as a main dish or complement sliced cold meat for a delicious, easy dinner. From Mueller's Spaghetti package.

1 medium onion, sliced
¼ cup olive oil
2 medium zucchini, sliced (about 6 cups)
3 cups diced tomatoes
½ tsp. salt
1 bay leaf

¼ tsp. pepper
¼ tsp. basil leaves
¼ tsp. oregano leaves
8 ounces Mueller's Spaghetti
Grated Parmesan cheese

In large skillet or pot, sauté onion in hot oil until crisp-tender. Add zucchini, tomatoes, salt, bay leaf, pepper, basil and oregano. Simmer covered for 15 minutes; uncover and simmer 10 minutes longer. Discard bay leaf. Meanwhile, cook spaghetti as directed on package; drain. Serve spaghetti topped with zucchini sauce and grated Parmesan cheese. Makes 4 to 6 servings.

Grant Street Pilaf

A perfect side dish for chicken, lamb or pork from the Dole Pineapple Chunks can.

1 20 ounce can Dole Pineapple Chunks, in syrup

2 Tbs. soy sauce
1 tsp. grated fresh ginger root

2 cups water
1 cup long-grain brown
  rice
½ tsp. rosemary
2 Tbs. butter

2 Tbs. chopped green
  onion
¼ cup toasted slivered
  almonds

Drain pineapple syrup into saucepan. Add water and bring to boil. Stir in rice and rosemary. Cover and simmer 35 to 45 minutes, until rice is tender and liquid is absorbed. Mix in pineapple chunks and remaining ingredients and heat through. Makes 4 to 6 servings.

Mushroom Pilaf

This delicious side dish was the star of a recent Fleischmann's Margarine advertisement. It's a great accompaniment to chicken or lamb.

2 cups sliced mushrooms
½ cup chopped onion
2 cloves garlic, crushed
2 Tbs. chopped parsley
1 tsp. basil leaves,
  crushed
⅛ tsp. pepper

2 Tbs. Fleischmann's
  Margarine
⅔ cup uncooked
  converted rice
1⅓ cups water
⅓ cup chopped toasted
  blanced almonds

Sauté mushrooms, onion, garlic, parsley, basil and pepper in margarine about 5 minutes, stirring frequently. Stir in rice and water. Bring to a boil over high heat. Cover; reduce heat and simmer until liquid is absorbed and rice is tender, about 25 minutes. Stir in almonds. Makes 7 servings.

Campbell's Scalloped Potatoes

You'll never be disappointed by curdled scalloped potatoes when you use this never-fail Campbell's recipe.

1 10¾-ounce can
  Campbell's Condensed
  Cream of Celery or
  Mushroom Soup
⅓ to ½ cup milk
¼ cup chopped parsley
  Dash pepper

4 cups thinly sliced
  potatoes
1 small onion, thinly
  sliced
1 Tbs. butter or margarine
  Dash paprika

Combine soup, milk, parsley and pepper. In 1½-quart casserole, arrange alternate layers of potatoes, onion and sauce. Dot top with butter; sprinkle with paprika. Cover; bake at 375°F. for 1 hour. Uncover; bake 15 minutes more or until potatoes are done. Makes about 3½ cups.

Campfire Potatoes

The Purity Cheese Company tells us that these Campfire Potatoes have been a consumer favorite ever since the recipe first appeared on their Smokey Sharp cheese package a decade ago.

½ cup chopped onion
2 Tbs. butter
1 Tbs. flour
½ tsp. salt
⅛ tsp. pepper
1 cup (4 ounces) shredded
  Hoffman's Smokey Sharp

¾ cup milk
1 12-ounce package
  frozen shredded hash
  brown potatoes

Sauté onions in butter or margarine. Place in shallow one-quart baking dish or small skillet, brushed with butter. Add flour, salt and pepper. Mix well. Add cheese. Pour milk over cheese. Top with frozen potatoes. Cover. Bake at 350°F. for 30 to 35 minutes, or until potatoes are completely thawed. Mix well. Return to oven uncovered and bake 15 to 20 minutes, or until golden brown. Makes 4 servings.

Candied Sweet Potatoes

Southerners unite! This is the real thing—this recipe for sweet potatoes has remained a popular standby on the Karo Dark Corn Syrup label for years.

1 cup Karo Dark Corn
   Syrup
½ cup firmly packed dark
   brown sugar
2 Tbs. corn oil margarine

12 medium sweet
   potatoes, cooked,
   peeled, halved
   lengthwise

In small saucepan, heat corn syrup, brown sugar and margarine to boiling; reduce heat and simmer 5 minutes. Pour ½ cup of the syrup into 13 × 9 × 2-inch baking dish. Arrange potatoes, overlapping if necessary, in syrup. Top with remaining syrup. Bake in 350°F. oven, basting often, for 20 minutes, until well glazed. Makes 12 servings.

Creamy Seasoned Noodles

Here's an easy way to cook noodles using Good Season's Italian Salad Dressing Mix.

1 8-ounce package wide egg noodles or spaghetti

1 envelope Good Season's Italian Salad Dressing Mix

½ cup heavy cream or evaporated milk

¼ cup butter or margarine

¼ cup grated Parmesan cheese

Chopped parsley, optional

Cook noodles as directed on package; drain well. Add remaining ingredients and toss lightly to blend thoroughly. Sprinkle with chopped parsley, if desired. Makes 4 cups or 8 servings.

Sautéed Wheatena

This unusual recipe is from the Wheatena box. Try it with lamb; it's delicious.

1 cup Wheatena

1 egg, beaten

1 tsp. salt

¼ cup butter or margarine

1 medium onion, diced

2 cups water

Combine Wheatena, egg and salt. In skillet, melt butter; sauté onion until golden. Add Wheatena mixture and water; mix well. Bring to boil; cover and cook over low heat until light in color, stirring occasionally. Cook about 10 to 12 minutes, until desired thickness. Makes about 5 to 6 servings.

Fried Wheatena

Down South we used to fry grits much like this. Try this variation without syrup as an accompaniment to roast chicken or duck.

1 cup Wheatena   1 tsp. salt
3½ cups water

Combine Wheatena, water and salt in large saucepan. Bring to rolling boil. Cook 5 minutes or until thick. Remove from heat; cool about 5 minutes. Pour into 9 × 5 × 3-inch loaf pan. Cover; chill until firm. Unmold; cut into 1-inch slices. Sauté, turning to brown on both sides. Serve hot with brown sugar or maple syrup. Makes 9 1-inch slices.

Note: Left-over Wheatena may also be used this way.

Boston Baked Beans

This genuine, old-time, real Baked Bean recipe is from the Grandma's Molasses label, where it was a fixture for years. This is the real thing, no instant nonsense allowed, so get out the bean pot, make up a batch of coleslaw and invite your friends for a Saturday-night feast.

1 lb. (2 cups) dried pea,   ¼ lb. salt pork
  marrow, Great Northern   ¾ cup Grandma's
  or navy beans   Unsulphured Molasses
2 quarts water   1 tsp. salt
1 onion, chopped   1 tsp. dry mustard

Rinse beans in cold water and drain. Place in large saucepan and add water. Bring to a boil and boil for 2 minutes. Remove from heat, cover loosely and let stand for 1 hour. Return to heat and bring to a boil;

cover and simmer gently over low heat for 1 hour, until beans are tender. Drain beans and reserve liquid. Turn beans into 2½-quart bean pot or casserole; add onion and mix lightly. Cut through surface of salt pork every ½ inch, making cuts about 1 inch deep. Bury pork in beans. Mix 2 cups reserved bean liquid with molasses, salt and dry mustard; pour over beans. Cover and bake in 300°F. oven for 5 to 6 hours. Check beans about once an hour and add additional bean liquid or water if the beans become dry; at the beginning of the cooking time the beans should be covered with liquid, and at the end of cooking the beans should be very moist and coated with syrupy liquid. Makes 8 servings.

4.
Salads
and Their
Dressings

I'll confess I love salads, perhaps because they are all too often culinary orphans and like all neglected orphans they flower with a little imagination and a bit of T.L.C.

A salad can make a meal. Pick one of the casserole dishes in this book, or any hearty main course, add a salad, and dinner is served; or the salad can *be* the meal. Take a Caesar salad, add crunchy rolls, a good dessert and coffee; who could ask for more for a perfect lunch or supper?

Salads are doubly important to you and your family because they provide the fresh uncooked fruits and vegetables we all need. There's been a lot of talk lately about the need for roughage in our diets. The surest and most pleasant way to consume sufficient roughage is to eat a generous serving of salad at least once a day. Fresh salad vegetables and fruits also provide important vitamins and minerals. Moreover, every healthy person requires some unsaturated fats, and the most flavorful way to add them to your diet is with a zesty salad dressing. A good salad rounds out the meal, adding contrasting flavor and texture to the main dish, complementing and enhancing the meat, chicken or fish you may be serving—deliciously! In fact, if your family doesn't eat salad, it's not because they don't like salads, but because the salad lacked inspiration. Look through these pages for the best-ever salads and dressings.

Included are the old favorites, such as Perfection and Under the Sea salads, along with a bevy of new ideas, plus a collection of salad dressings that will turn anyone into a salad buff. I've tried every one and I would be hard pressed to pick the best. Every one is a triumph of flavor, a great addition to any cook's repertoire. Perhaps, too, you will find, as I did, that these recipes will lead to other new ideas, fruits and vegetable combinations you hadn't thought of before, or new ways to use a dressing you particularly liked. I hope so, for salad making is fun, easy, quick, and a great way to add sparkling new flavor at low cost to every meal you serve.

Caesar Salad

The Caesar Salad was created at Caesar's Bar and Grill in Tijuana, Mexico, just South of the Border near the fragrant lemon groves of California. Caesar's famous salad has been acclaimed by epicures the world over. The Sunkist Lemon people printed this classic in their advertising a decade ago. It's a year-round favorite.

1 clove garlic, crushed
⅔ cup olive oil
4 quarts romaine lettuce, chilled, torn (about 3 medium heads)
1 tsp. salt
 Freshly ground pepper
1 Tbs. Worcestershire sauce

1 egg
3 to 4 Tbs. fresh squeezed lemon juice
2 Tbs. wine vinegar
6 to 8 anchovy fillets, chopped, optional
½ cup grated Parmesan cheese
1 cup croutons

Add garlic to oil; let stand overnight. Discard garlic. Place romaine in large salad bowl. Sprinkle with salt, pepper and Worcestershire sauce. Coddle egg for 1½ minutes; break into middle of salad. Pour lemon juice and wine vinegar over egg. Toss lightly to mix well. Add remaining ingredients, tossing after each addition. Adjust seasonings if necessary. Serve immediately. Makes 8 servings.

Cannellini Chef's Salad

From Progresso Foods, a meal-sized salad to serve with Italian bread and a glass of Chianti.

2 cans (20 ounces each) Progresso Cannellini Beans
⅓ cup olive oil
3 Tbs. wine vinegar
1 clove garlic, minced
2 tsps. oregano leaves, crumbled
1 tsp. salt
¼ tsp. ground black pepper
3 quarts torn iceberg lettuce
¼ lb. sliced ham, slivered
2 ounces sliced salami, slivered
¼ lb. Mozzarella cheese, slivered
¼ cup sliced roasted peppers

Drain cannellini beans thoroughly. Meanwhile, in a medium bowl mix together oil, vinegar, garlic, oregano, salt and black pepper. Stir in cannellini beans. Place lettuce in a very large bowl. Spoon beans in a circle close to side of bowl. Arrange ham, salami, cheese and roasted peppers in any desired pattern over the lettuce. Toss just before serving. Makes 6 portions.

Salmon Salad on Avocado Half Shells

A delicious new way to serve canned salmon, from the Avocado Advisory Board's advertising pages.

3 California avocados
Lettuce
1 15½-ounce can or 2 7¾-ounce cans salmon, chilled
2 Tbs. sliced green onion
½ cup sliced celery
Lemon-Parsley Dressing

Halve, pit and peel avocados, arrange on lettuce-lined plates. Drain salmon and separate into chunks with a fork. Toss salmon lightly with celery and green onions. Fill avocados with salmon mixture. Drizzle with Lemon-Parsley Dressing.

Lemon-Parsley Dressing: Combine ⅔ cup oil, 3 Tbs. lemon juice, one clove of minced garlic, ¼ tsp. dry mustard, ½ tsp. salt, ⅛ tsp. pepper and 1 Tbs. minced parsley in jar. Cover and shake until blended. Makes approximately 1 cup dressing.

Sunkist Onion and Orange Salad

This was a Hollywood favorite back in the days when Greta Garbo was queen of the film capital. It was and still is one of the best salads ever devised.

1 large mild flavored onion
2 large Sunkist Oranges, peeled
¼ tsp. salt
⅛ tsp. oregano, crushed
¼ cup salad oil
1 Tbs. fresh squeezed orange juice
1 Tbs. fresh squeezed lemon juice
Lettuce
2 Tbs. ripe black olives, sliced
Coarsely ground black pepper

Cut onion into 8 thin slices and oranges into 6 slices each. Place in glass dish; marinate for 15 minutes in mixture of salt, oregano, oil, orange and lemon juice. Arrange in a row on individual beds of crisp lettuce, alternating 3 orange slices and 2 onion slices per serving. Top with sliced olives and spoon over remaining marinade. Add a generous sprinkling of fresh ground pepper. Makes 4 servings.

Under-The-Sea-Salad

This recipe is pre–World War II vintage, and the Jell-O people tell us it remains a consistent favorite to this day.

1 16-ounce can pear
halves
1 3-ounce package Jell-O
Lime Gelatin
¼ tsp. salt
1 cup boiling water

1 Tbs. lemon juice
2 3-ounce packages
cream cheese
⅛ tsp. cinnamon
Chicory or watercress
Mayonnaise, optional

Drain pears, reserving ¾ cup of the syrup. Dice pears and set aside. Dissolve Jell-O and salt in boiling water. Add reserved syrup and lemon juice. Pour 1¼ cups into an 8 × 4-inch loaf pan. Chill until set but not firm, about 1 hour. Meanwhile, soften cheese until creamy. Very slowly blend in remaining gelatin, beating until smooth. Blend in pears. Spoon into pan. Chill until firm, about 4 hours. Unmold and garnish with chicory or watercress. Serve with mayonnaise, if desired. Makes about 3½ cups or 6 servings.

Note: Recipe may be doubled, using a 9 × 5-inch loaf pan. Recipe may be chilled in a 4-cup mold.

Cool 'N Creamy Coleslaw

If you are tired of "just coleslaw" whip up this special molded version. It's been a favorite since the recipe appeared on the Knox Gelatine package decades ago.

2 envelopes Knox
Unflavored Gelatine
2 Tbs. sugar
1¾ cups boiling water
1⅓ cups mayonnaise
¼ cup lemon juice

4 cups shredded
cabbage
1 cup shredded carrots
¼ cup finely chopped
onion

In large bowl, mix Knox Unflavored Gelatine and sugar; add boiling water and stir until gelatin is completely dissolved. With wire whisk or rotary beater, blend in mayonnaise and lemon juice; chill until mixture is consistency of unbeaten egg whites. Stir in cabbage, carrots, and onion; pour into 11 × 7-inch pan and chill until firm. To serve, cut into squares. Makes about 8 servings.

Cranberry Apple Waldorf

Back in the Thirties Christmas wasn't Christmas at our house without this molded cranberry salad. The recipe was on the Knox Gelatine box for years and it's still festive and delicious.

3 envelopes Knox Unflavored Gelatine	3½ cups cranberry juice cocktail
⅓ cup sugar	1 cup chopped apple
1 cup boiling water	½ cup chopped celery
	⅓ cup chopped walnuts

In large bowl, mix Knox Unflavored Gelatine and sugar; add boiling water and stir until gelatin is completely dissolved. Add cranberry juice; chill until mixture is consistency of unbeaten egg whites. Fold in apple, celery and walnuts; pour into 8- or 9-inch square pan and chill until firm. To serve, cut into squares, serve as a relish. Makes about 8 servings.

Perfection Salad

Birth of a classic recipe . . . In *1905*, Charles Knox ran a cookery contest, and Fannie Farmer was one of the judges. Third prize, a sewing machine, was awarded to Mrs. John E. Cooke of New Castle, Pennsylvania, who submitted a recipe she called Perfection Salad. The recipe was widely distributed and was greeted with such enthusiasm it is now considered an American classic.

1 envelope Knox Unflavored Gelatine	½ cup shredded cabbage, red or green
¼ cup sugar	1 cup chopped celery
½ tsp. salt	1 pimiento, cut in small pieces, or 2 Tbs. chopped sweet red or green pepper
1¼ cups water, divided	
¼ cup vinegar	
1 Tbs. lemon juice	

Mix Knox Unflavored Gelatine, sugar and salt thoroughly in a small saucepan. Add ½ cup of water. Place over low heat, stirring constantly until gelatin is dissolved. Remove from heat and stir in remaining ¾ cup of water, vinegar and lemon juice. Chill mixture to unbeaten egg white consistency. Fold in shredded cabbage, celery and pimiento or pepper. Turn in a 2-cup mold or individual molds and chill until firm. Unmold on serving plate and garnish with salad greens. Serve with favorite salad dressing.

Variations:

Pineapple Perfection Salad: Substitute ¾ cup canned pineapple juice for ¾ cup of the water. Reduce sugar to 2 Tbs.

Olive Perfection Salad: Substitute ½ cup chopped ripe olives for the pimiento.

Peanut Perfection: Substitute ½ cup chopped peanuts for the celery.

Cucumber and Onion Perfection: Substitute ½ cup chopped cucumbers and 1 small onion, chopped, for the celery.

Cauliflower Perfection Salad: Substitute ½ cup finely cut crisp raw cauliflower and 2 Tbs. chopped green pepper for ½ cup of the chopped celery.

Jello Artichoke Salad

A beautifully molded salad to grace the most elegant buffet table. Dreamed up by the cooks in General Foods kitchens.

1 9-ounce package Birds Eye Deluxe Artichoke Hearts
1 cup (about ¼ lb.) sliced fresh mushrooms
1 cup prepared Good Seasons Italian Salad Dressing
1 3-ounce package Jell-O (Lemon or Lime)
1 cup boiling water
2 tsps. vinegar
¾ cup cold water
1 Tbs. sliced pimiento

Cook artichoke hearts as directed on package. Drain and combine with mushrooms in a bowl. Pour dressing over vegetables and allow to marinate at least 1 hour. Drain, reserving marinade. Dissolve Jello-O in boiling water. Add vinegar and cold water. Chill until thickened. Fold in the drained mushrooms and artichoke hearts, and pimiento. Pour into a 4-cup mold. Chill until firm, about 4 hours. Makes 3⅓ cups or 6 salads.

Note: If desired, reserved marinade can be combined with mayonnaise and used as a dressing for the salad.

Jell-O Molded Vegetable Relish

A zippy relish that is really a salad, especially nice for a summer luncheon mainstay. Start with a soup, end with a special dessert, and it's a party!

1 3-ounce package Jello-O
   (Lemon or Lime) Gelatin
¾ tsp. salt
1 cup boiling water
¾ cup cold water

2 Tbs. vinegar
2 tsps. grated onion
   Dash of pepper
   Vegetable combinations*

Dissolve Jell-O and salt in boiling water. Add cold water, vinegar, grated onion, and pepper. Chill until thickened. Fold in your choice of vegetable combination. Pour into individual molds for salad or small molds for relish. Chill until firm, about 3 hours. Unmold. For salad, serve with crisp lettuce and garnish with mayonnaise, if desired. Makes about 3 cups or 6 salad servings or 8 relish servings.

*Vegetable Combinations:

½ cup each finely chopped cabbage, celery, and carrots, and 3 Tbs. finely chopped green pepper.

¾ cup each finely chopped cabbage and celery, ¼ cup finely chopped green pepper, and 2 Tbs. diced pimiento.

¾ cup each finely chopped cabbage and celery, ½ cup chopped pickle, and 2 Tbs. diced pimiento.

¾ cup each drained cooked peas and diced celery and ½ cup finely chopped cabbage.

1 cup finely chopped cabbage, ½ cup sliced stuffed olives; omit salt.

⅔ cup grated carrots and ¼ cup finely chopped green pepper.

Summer Salad

A great salad for a summer lunch or supper, the recipe first appeared on the back of Armour's Golden Star Ham and I've been serving it ever since. Try it with hot orange muffins and iced tea—it's beautiful!

Leaf lettuce
1 29-ounce can peach halves, drained
1 17-ounce can pear halves, drained
1 14¼-ounce can sliced pineapple, drained
1 lb. Armour Golden Star Ham, thinly sliced
Cream cheese
Chopped walnuts
Canned blueberries
Whole strawberries

Dressing: ¾ cup dairy sour cream, 1 Tbs. horseradish mustard, 2 tsps. sugar, 1 tsp. lemon juice. Combine ingredients; chill. Serve with salad.

Salad: Line platter with lettuce; arrange peaches, pears, pineapple slices and ham on lettuce. Roll cream cheese into balls; roll in walnuts. Arrange cream cheese balls with pineapple. Fill each peach half with blueberries; garnish each pear half with a strawberry. Makes 4 servings.

Poppy Seed Dressing

Sunkist Lemon Growers suggest this creamy-smooth dressing for fruit salad.

½ cup sugar
1 tsp. salt
1 tsp. dry mustard
1 tsp. fresh grated lemon peel
1 tsp. finely minced onion
⅓ cup fresh squeezed lemon juice
¾ cup salad oil
Few drops red food coloring
1 Tbs. poppy seeds

Combine all ingredients except food coloring and poppy seeds in electric blender or covered container. Cover and blend or shake until thoroughly mixed. Tint mixture to a delicate pink color with a drop or two of red food coloring. Stir in poppy seeds. Chill before serving with fresh fruits in season. Makes 1½ cups.

Old-Fashioned Potato Salad

This is the real thing! Apparently customers agree. They have been asking for the recipe since it originally appeared.

1 cup Hellmann's (or Best Foods) Real Mayonnaise	2 hard-cooked eggs, chopped
1 cup minced onion	3 lbs. potatoes, cooked, peeled, cubed (about 6 cups)
3 Tbs. white vinegar	
2 tsps. salt	
¼ tsp. pepper	2 cups sliced celery

In large bowl stir together mayonnaise, onion, vinegar, salt, pepper and eggs. Add potatoes and celery; toss to coat well. Cover; refrigerate for at least 4 hours. If desired, sprinkle with paprika. Makes about 8 cups.

Avocado Dressing for Fruit Salads

The fruit salad dressing supreme, this recipe first appeared in the Avocado Advisory Board's advertising in 1965. It's been an "asked-for" special ever since. It gives an added dimension to a favorite fruit salad, making it more of a "meal." Serve with hot honey buns and loads of fresh coffee.

3 avocados, puréed	1½ tsps. salt
1 cup sour cream	2 Tbs. lime juice

Combine all ingredients and chill 30 minutes. Serve with green or fruit salad. Makes 3 cups.

Tomato French Dressing

Here it is! That classic French Dressing recipe that appeared on Campbell's Tomato Soup cans back before World War II. It's a "secret" recipe of many great cooks.

1 10¾-ounce can
  Campbell's Condensed
  Tomato Soup

½ cup salad oil
¼ cup vinegar
½ tsp. dry mustard

In covered jar or shaker, combine ingredients; shake well before using. (Or mix in an electric blender.) Makes about 1½ cups.

Variations: To 1 recipe of Tomato French Dressing add any one of the following:

4 slices bacon, cooked
  and crumbled
¼ cup crumbled blue
  cheese

1 medium clove garlic,
  minced
¼ cup sweet pickle relish

HELLMANN'S (OR BEST FOODS) FOUR BEST

A few years ago a series of recipes was featured in the Hellmann's advertising. Here are four of the best, two of which include Dannon Yogurt. I think you will enjoy them all.

Pecan Dressing

⅓ cup Hellmann's (or Best
  Foods) Real Mayonnaise
⅓ cup chopped pecans

¼ cup Karo Light Corn
  Syrup
1 cup (8 ounces) Dannon
  Plain Yogurt

Stir together first 3 ingredients. Fold in yogurt. Chill. Serve over fruit. Makes 1½ cups.

Thousand Island Dressing

⅓ cup Hellmann's (or Best Foods) Real Mayonnaise
1 hard-cooked egg, finely chopped
½ cup chili sauce
1 Tbs. chopped pimiento-stuffed olive

1 Tbs. chopped dill pickle
1 tsp. grated onion
1 8-ounce cup Dannon Plain Yogurt

Stir together first 6 ingredients. Fold in yogurt. Chill. Makes 2 cups.

California-Style Blue Cheese Dressing

1 cup Hellmann's (or Best Foods) Real Mayonnaise
1 4-ounce package blue cheese, crumbled (1 cup)

¼ cup dry white wine
1 Tbs. grated onion
4 to 5 drops hot pepper sauce

Combine all ingredients. Cover; chill 1 hour. Serve over fresh-cooked chilled vegetables or tossed salad. Makes 1⅔ cups.

Russian Dressing

½ cup Hellmann's (or Best Foods) Real Mayonnaise
⅓ cup chili sauce

2 Tbs. milk
1 Tbs. sweet relish

Combine all ingredients. Cover; chill 1 hour. Serve over greens. Makes 1 cup.

5.
All
Manner
of
Breads

"The true measure of a good cook is the bread that graces the table." Time was when baking was a "chancy" thing: balky ovens, uncertain yeast, flour that varied from package to package; all led to the old wives' tale that only highly skilled cooks could bake their own breads. But today we have all the "chance" taken out of bread baking, leaving only the pleasure of making and the double pleasure of enjoying.

Like all our recipes, these for pancakes, muffins, breads and rolls are literally fail-proof. Whether you decide to whip up some old-fashioned bran muffins, a loaf of fragrant white bread, or flaky croissants, they will unfailingly rise to glorious culinary heights.

Actually, it was hard work trying to decide which recipes to include here, there were so many great ones. Finally the decision was made to give you the basic favorites—the very ones you have requested—then a sprinkling of variety for spice. There are Caraway Rye Rolls, great for a picnic supper; Maple Pecan Rolls to accompany hot coffee for breakfast or a fruit salad luncheon; Banana and Pumpkin Breads for tea and of course sticky buns, for what would a chapter on bread be without these?

If you are new to bread baking, I hope you will try your hand at one or all of these recipes. I'll guarantee you will be so pleased with your success you'll seldom buy ordinary bread again. As for you "old hands," here are the favorites you've asked for, and as old friends I know you will welcome them. These are the breads you like to make, sent to you with the good wishes of other good cooks, the talented people who have taken the suspense out of baking and replaced it with pleasure. Happy baking!

Quick Buckwheat Cakes

Old-fashioned buckwheat pancakes from the back of Elam's Pure Buckwheat Flour box, so special they deserve special treatment. Try real maple syrup and sweet butter or fresh berries and sour cream. Make lots of coffee!

2 cups Elam's Pure
Buckwheat Flour
1 tsp. baking powder
¾ tsp. salt
½ tsp. baking soda
2½ cups milk
¼ cup cooking oil or
melted shortening

Combine first four ingredients in bowl; mix well. Add milk and oil or melted shortening; stir until smooth. Stir batter down before using each time. For each pancake, pour about ¼ cup batter onto hot, lightly greased griddle. Bake until top is covered with bubbles and edges look cooked. Turn and brown second side. Makes about 16 cakes, 4 inches in diameter.

Buttermilk Cakes: Follow recipe for Quick Buckwheat Cakes above and change as follows: Increase baking soda to 1½ tsps. Substitute 3 cups buttermilk or sour milk for 2½ cups sweet milk. Makes about 18 cakes, 4½ inches in diameter, 6 servings of 3 pancakes each.

Banana Bran Bread

Elam's have been printing this recipe for Banana Bread on their Bran package for over a decade. It's a classic the customers won't let them drop.

⅓ cup shortening
⅔ cup honey
¾ cup Elam's Bran
2 eggs
1 cup ripe banana pulp
1½ cups all-purpose flour
2¼ tsps. baking powder
½ tsp. salt

Thoroughly blend the first five ingredients in a bowl. Sift together and add flour, baking powder and salt. Pour into a greased 8½ × 4½ × 2½-inch loaf pan. Bake at 350°F. for 1 hour, until done. Cool on wire rack. Makes 1 loaf.

Our Best Bran Muffins

Your mother probably made muffins from this old-timer. The recipe for Best Bran Muffins first appeared on Kellogg's All-Bran cereal box in 1926.

1¼ cups all-purpose flour
3 tsps. baking powder
½ tsp. salt
½ cup sugar
1½ cups Kellogg's All-Bran cereal or Bran Buds cereal

1¼ cups milk
1 egg
⅓ cup shortening or vegetable oil

Stir together flour, baking powder, salt and sugar. Set aside. Measure All-Bran cereal and milk into large mixing bowl. Stir to combine. Let stand 1 to 2 minutes, until cereal is softened. Add egg and shortening. Beat well. Add flour mixture, stirring only until combined. Portion batter evenly into 12 greased 2½-inch muffin-pan cups. Bake in 400°F. oven for about 25 minutes or until lightly browned. Makes 12 muffins.

Variations: 3 cups Kellogg's Raisin Bran cereal or 2½ cups Kellogg's 40% Bran Flakes cereal may be substituted for All-Bran cereal.

Pumpkin Bread

This is a long-time favorite recipe from Del Monte, especially good to have on hand for holiday entertaining. Extra easy too! It's been on their pumpkin can label since 1969.

3 cups sugar
1 cup salad oil
4 eggs, beaten
1 16-ounce can Del Monte Pumpkin
3½ cups sifted flour
2 tsps. baking soda

2 tsps. salt
1 tsp. baking powder
1 tsp. nutmeg
1 tsp. allspice
1 tsp. cinnamon
½ tsp. ground cloves
⅔ cup water

Cream sugar and oil. Add eggs and pumpkin; mix well. Sift together flour, baking soda, salt, baking powder, nutmeg, allspice, cinnamon and cloves. Add to pumpkin mixture alternately with water. Mix well after each addition. Pour into 2 well-greased and floured 9 × 5-inch loaf pans. Bake at 350°F. for 1½ hours, until loaves test done. Let stand for 10 minutes. Remove from pans to cool. Makes 2 loaves.

Super Wheat Germ Zucchini Bread

Super good-tasting and super-good for you. This Wheat Germ Zucchini Bread made its debut on the Kretschmer jar in 1977. Its flavor comes from the honest taste of wheat. Try it hot, spread with soft butter for a special "coffee-break" treat.

1¼ cups Kretschmer Wheat Germ, regular
3 cups flour
3 tsps. baking powder
1 tsp. salt
2 tsps. cinnamon
1 cup chopped nuts

2 eggs
1¾ cups sugar
2 tsps. vanilla
⅔ cup cooking oil
3 cups (about 3 medium-size) grated zucchini

Mix together wheat germ, flour, baking powder, salt, cinnamon and nuts. Beat eggs until light-colored and fluffy. Beat in sugar, vanilla and oil. Stir in zucchini. Gradually stir in wheat-germ mixture. Turn into 2 greased and floured 8½ × 4½ × 2½-inch loaf pans. Bake in 350°F. oven for 1 hour, until a pick inserted into center comes out clean. If using glass pans, bake at 325°F. Cool for 5 to 10 minutes. Remove from pans and cool on rack. Makes 2 loaves.

Dilly Casserole Bread

The most memorable bread recipe from all of the Pillsbury Bake-Off Contests! The soft moist texture, the delicate dill and onion flavor and its easy preparation truly make it a prize-winner.

1 pkg. active dry yeast
¼ cup very warm water (105°F. to 115°F.)
1 cup creamed cottage cheese
2 Tbs. sugar
1 Tbs. instant minced onion
2 tsps. dill seed
1 tsp. salt
¼ tsp. soda
1 Tbs. margarine or butter
1 egg
2½ cups Pillsbury's Best All Purpose or Unbleached Flour*
Margarine or butter, softened
Salt

In large bowl, soften yeast in warm water. In small saucepan, heat cottage cheese to lukewarm. Combine cottage cheese, sugar, onion, dill seed, 1 tsp. salt, soda, margarine and egg with softened yeast. Lightly spoon flour into measuring cup; level off; add 1½ cups flour. Beat for 2 minutes at medium speed. By hand, stir in

* For use with Pillsbury's Best Self-Rising Flour, omit salt and soda.

remaining 1 cup flour. Mix thoroughly. Cover; let rise in warm place until light and doubled in size, 50 to 60 minutes.

Generously grease (not oil) 8-inch round 1½- or 2-qt. casserole. Stir down dough; turn into greased casserole. Let rise in warm place until light and doubled in size, 30 to 40 minutes. Heat oven to 350°F. Bake for 40 to 50 minutes, until golden brown. Immediately remove from pan. Brush with soft margarine and sprinkle with salt. Makes 1 loaf.

In High Altitude: Above 3500 feet, bake at 357°F. for 35 to 40 minutes.

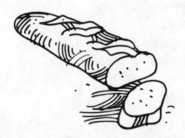

Wheat Germ White Bread

An old-fashioned nutty-flavored wheat germ bread from the label of Elam's Unbleached White Flour with Wheat Germ. Just try a slice spread with sweet butter!

1¼ cup milk, scalded	¼ cup warm water
1½ Tbs. honey	(105–115°F.)
1¼ tsp. salt	3⅓ cups (about) Elam's
2 tsps. cooking oil, soft	Unbleached White
shortening or butter	Flour with Wheat Germ
1 ¼-ounce package	
active dry yeast	

Combine first 4 ingredients in bowl; mix and cool to lukewarm. Dissolve yeast in warm water. Stir into milk mixture. Stir a small amount of flour into liquids at a time, adding flour as needed to make a stiff dough. Beat well after each addition. Turn dough onto lightly floured board; knead until dough is smooth and elastic. Place dough in well-greased bowl; turn dough to grease top and cover with damp towel. Let rise in warm place until double in size. Punch down; let rise again until double in size. Punch down; let rest for 10 minutes. Shape dough into loaf. Place in greased 9 × 5 × 3-inch loaf pan; brush top of loaf with soft shortening, butter or cooking oil. Cover; let rise until almost double in size. Bake in moderate oven (375°F.) until done, about 40 minutes. Makes 1 large loaf.

Note: If desired, above recipe may be doubled and shaped into 3 loaves; place in 3 greased 8½ × 4½ × 2⅝-inch loaf pans. Reduce baking time to 35 minutes.

Basic Sweet Dough

For coffee cakes, cinnamon buns or just faintly sweet dinner rolls, this recipe from the box of Elam's Unbleached White Flour with Wheat Germ can't be beaten for flavor and texture.

½ cup milk, scalded
⅓ cup honey or sugar
1½ tsps. salt
¼ cup butter
1 egg, beaten slightly
½ tsp. grated lemon rind
1 ¼-ounce package active dry yeast

¼ cup warm water (105–115°F.)
2¾ cups (about) Elam's Unbleached White Flour with Wheat Germ

Combine first 4 ingredients in bowl; mix and cool to lukewarm. Stir in egg and lemon rind. Dissolve yeast in warm water. Stir into milk mixture. Stir flour into liquids, a little at a time, adding flour as needed to make a stiff dough. Beat well after each addition. Turn dough onto lightly floured board; knead until dough is smooth and elastic. Place dough in well-greased bowl; turn dough to grease top. Cover with damp towel; let rise in warm place until double in size. Punch down; let rest for 10 minutes. Prepare as directed for one of the sweet breads listed below.

Cinnamon Rolls: Roll sweet dough into an 8 × 10-inch rectangle; brush 2 Tbs. melted butter over dough. Combine and mix ½ cup sugar or turbinado and 2 tsps. cinnamon; sprinkle evenly over dough. Roll up as for jelly roll, starting with long side. Cut roll crosswise into slices 1 inch thick. Place, cut side down, in greased 13 × 9 × 2-inch baking pan. Cover; let rise in warm place until double in size. Bake in moderate oven (350°F.) about 30 minutes, until done and browned. Frost with a confectioners' sugar icing, if desired. Makes 18 rolls.

Butterscotch Pecan Rolls: Melt 3 Tbs. butter in saucepan; add ⅓ cup brown sugar, packed, and ¼ cup honey or corn syrup. Place over low heat until sugar melts and mixture is smooth. Pour into buttered 13 × 9 × 2-inch baking pan; spread in even layer over bottom of pan. Sprinkle ⅓ cup coarsely chopped pecans over butterscotch mixture. Proceed as for Cinnamon Rolls above, except substitute ¾ cup (packed) light brown sugar for granulated sugar or turbinado and omit cinnamon. Sprinkle ⅓ cup chopped pecans over sugar before rolling. Immediately upon removing from oven, invert pan on rack over a sheet of aluminum foil or a buttered baking sheet. Let stand 1 or 2 minutes before removing from pan. Makes 18 rolls.

Coffee Cake: Prepare Basic Sweet Dough using above recipe and change as follows: Increase honey or sugar to ½ cup. Roll dough into a 14 × 10 inch-rectangle. Brush 1 Tbs. melted butter over surface. Combine and mix ¼ cup brown sugar, packed, 2 tsps. cinnamon, ¾ cup chopped pecans and 1 cup raisins or coarsely chopped mixed candied fruit.* Sprinkle evenly over dough. Roll up as for jelly roll, starting with long side. Seal long edge. Form into a ring, seam side down, on greased baking sheet. Fasten ends together by moistening and pinching edges together. Using scissors cut two-thirds of the way through the ring to center at 1½-inch intervals. Turn each section slightly to one side. Cover; let rise until double in size. Bake in moderate oven (350°F.) until done and browned, about 30 minutes. (Cover loosely with aluminum foil if ring browns too quickly.) If desired, drizzle favorite confectioners' sugar icing over ring while warm. Makes 1 large coffee ring.

Parkerhouse Rolls

These rolls were originally created by the chef of Boston's famed Parker House Hotel in 1905.

Prepare one recipe of Wheat Germ Hot Rolls dough. Instead of dividing dough and shaping into balls, roll

---

* If using candied fruit, substitute finely shredded orange rind for cinnamon.

it ½-inch thick on a lightly floured board. Cut into rounds, using a floured 2½- or 3-inch cookie cutter. Brush tops of rounds with melted butter. Using back of dinner knife blade make an indentation across each round of dough to one side of center and fold round in half. Press edges together lightly. Arrange rolls close together in rows on greased baking sheet. Brush tops with melted butter. Cover; let rise until double in size. Bake in moderate oven (375°F.) until done and brown, 15 to 18 minutes. Brush tops with melted butter. Makes 20 to 24 rolls.

Stollen

Real honest-to-goodness stollen, not just coffee cake; here's the European recipe faithfully tested by the Blue Diamond Almond test kitchens. Perfect for Sunday brunch or a special holiday breakfast.

1 package dry yeast
¼ cup lukewarm water
⅔ cup milk
½ cup butter or margarine
¼ cup sugar
1 egg
½ tsp. almond extract
½ tsp. salt
3¼ to 3½ cups sifted all-purpose flour

¾ cup Blue Diamond Blanched Slivered Almonds, toasted
1 cup golden raisins
½ cup halved candied cherries
Confectioners' sugar icing

Dissolve yeast in water. Scald milk; add butter and sugar and stir until sugar is dissolved. Cool to lukewarm. Beat egg and add to milk mixture with yeast, almond extract and salt. Stir in 2 cups flour and beat until smooth. Stir in almonds, raisins and cherries. Add remaining flour, and mix until smooth. Cover and let rise in warm place until doubled in bulk, about 1½ hours. Punch down; knead lightly, and pat to 12-inch circle. Fold in half and press edges together firmly. Place on greased baking sheet. Brush top with melted butter. Let rise ½ hour in warm place. Bake in moderate (350°F.) oven for about 30 minutes. Spread top with icing while warm. Makes 1 large loaf.

Crumb Coffee Cake

I like this best made with pecans and served warm with lots of hot, fresh coffee! From the Domino Sugar carton back in 1968.

Topping:

⅓ cup firmly packed Domino Light Brown Sugar

3 Tbs. all-purpose flour

1 tsp. cinnamon

2 scant Tbs. soft butter or margarine

½ cup chopped nuts, optional

Combine brown sugar, flour and cinnamon in small mixing bowl. With pastry blender, blend butter into mixture thoroughly. Add nuts. Set aside.

Cake:

2 cups sifted all-purpose flour

2¼ tsps. double-acting baking powder

¾ cup Domino Superfine Sugar

¾ tsp. salt

2 eggs, well beaten

½ cup milk

½ cup salad oil

Sift together flour, baking powder, sugar and salt into mixing bowl. Combine beaten eggs, milk and oil. Stir liquid ingredients into dry ingredients until barely blended. Turn batter into greased 9-inch square cake pan. Spoon crumb topping over batter. Bake in 400°F. oven for 25 to 30 minutes, until done. Makes 9 3-inch squares.

6.
The
Very
Best Pies

We Americans simply love pies. Our fondness for them dates back to the English settlers who founded Colonial America, for pies are as old as England itself. Our New England ancestors used native apples and the Indian gift of pumpkin for those early desserts, but pie-making was by no means limited to those first fruits. Moving westward, our pioneer families adopted local fruits to make mouth-watering fresh peach and plum pies. Sour cherries, blackberries and rhubarb, too, lent their tart-sweet taste to flaky pastry. Hoosier housewives created shoofly pie with dark sweet molasses, while Southern cooks concocted those made-in-heaven chocolate pies and that ultimate in glorious calorie-abandon, the pecan pie.

As for lemon pie, it knows no geographic limitations. Created at the turn of the century, lemon pie remains second only to chocolate cake as our all-time favorite dessert.

But many a cook has shied away from pie-making, afraid that special skills were needed to make a perfect pie. If you are one of them, hesitate no longer. This chapter has all of your favorites to make the results as certain as the rising sun, plus a handy fruit-pie chart.

Even pastry making, that sometimes forbidding art, has lost its terrors; flaky unbaked shells are available in every supermarket, and dependable pie-crust mixes are easily at hand. Also included here is a never-fail pie-crust recipe. So make your own pastry, use a mix or a ready-to-bake shell, whatever suits your time, your skill or your fancy, but do go ahead and delight your family and guests with a real, honest-to-goodness, homemade pie. No other dessert is as dear to the hearts of all of us than freshly made pie.

Libby's Famous Pumpkin Pie

For seventy-five years this has been America's favorite pumpkin pie recipe and it is without doubt the best.

2 eggs, slightly beaten
1 16-ounce can Libby's Solid Pack Pumpkin
¾ cup sugar
½ tsp. salt
1 tsp. cinnamon
½ tsp. ginger
¼ tsp. cloves
1⅔ cups (13 fluid ounces) evaporated milk or light cream
1 9-inch unbaked pie shell with high fluted edge* **

Mix filling ingredients in order given. Pour into pie shell. Bake in preheated 425°F. oven for 15 minutes. Reduce temperature to 350°F. and continue baking for 45 minutes, until knife inserted in center of pie filling comes out clean. Cool. Garnish with whipped cream, if desired. Makes one 9-inch pie.

Crunchy Pecan Topping: In a small bowl, mix 1 cup coarsely chopped pecans with ⅔ cup firmly packed light brown sugar. Drizzle with 3 Tbs. melted butter or margarine; stir until uniformly moistened. Sprinkle over completely cooled pumpkin pie. Broil about 5 inches from heat for 1 to 2 minutes, until topping is bubbly. Serve while warm. Or, let cool, then garnish with whipped cream or dessert topping and extra pecan halves. Tops one 9-inch pie.

* If using regular frozen pie shells, recipe fills two. Bake on cookie sheet in preheated 425°F. oven for 15 minutes. Reduce heat to 350°F. and continue baking for about 30 minutes, until pies test done with knife, as noted above.

** If using deep-dish frozen pie shells, recipe fills one. Let shell thaw for ten minutes; then pinch edge so that it stands ½ inch above rim of pan. Bake filled pie on cookie sheet in preheated 425°F. oven for 15 minutes. Reduce heat to 350°F.; continue baking for about 50 minutes, until pie tests done with knife, as noted above.

Creamy Orange Pumpkin Pie

Here's another version of that famous Libby Pumpkin Pie. Gossamer light and delicately orange flavored, it made an instant hit when Libby added the recipe to its Solid Pack Pumpkin label several years ago.

1 9-inch frozen deep-dish
   pie shell
1 cup sugar
1 envelope unflavored
   gelatine
1 tsp. pumpkin pie spice
½ tsp. salt
1 can (13 fluid ounces)
   evaporated milk

2 eggs, separated
1 can (16 ounces) Libby's
   Solid Pack Pumpkin
½ cup orange marmalade
½ cup chopped pecans or
   shredded coconut

Bake pie shell according to package directions. Stir together ½ cup sugar, gelatine, pumpkin pie spice and salt in 2-quart saucepan. Add evaporated milk. Heat, stirring constantly, to boil; remove from heat. Beat egg yolks. Pour a portion of hot mixture into beaten egg yolks. Pour egg mixture back into saucepan. Mix well. Heat, stirring constantly, until mixture thickens. Remove from heat. Stir in pumpkin and orange marmalade. Chill until mixture mounds from spoon. Beat egg whites until foamy; gradually beat in remaining ½ cup sugar until stiff peaks form; fold into pumpkin mixture. Pour into baked pie shell. Top with pecans or coconut. Chill until set. Makes one 9-inch pie.

Pecan Pie

This recipe for pecan pie was printed on the Karo label in 1945. Today, after more than thirty years, it is still one of the most popular.

3 eggs
1 cup Karo Light or Dark Corn Syrup
1 cup sugar
2 Tbs. corn oil margarine, melted

1 tsp. vanilla
⅛ tsp. salt
1 cup pecans
1 9-inch unbaked pastry shell

Beat eggs slightly in a small bowl with mixer at medium speed. Beat in corn syrup, sugar, margarine, vanilla and salt. Stir in pecans. Pour filling into pastry shell. Bake in 350°F. oven 55 to 65 minutes or until knife inserted halfway between center and edge comes out clean. Cool. If desired, serve with whipped cream. Makes one 9-inch pie.

Lemon Meringue Pie

The century was young, the horseless carriage was making a tentative appearance and ladies' skirts still swept the ground in the early 1900s when this classic recipe was printed on the Argo Corn Starch package.

1 cup sugar
3 Tbs. Argo Corn Starch
1½ cups cold water
3 egg yolks, slightly beaten
1 lemon's grated rind

¼ cup lemon juice
1 Tbs. margarine
1 9-inch baked pastry shell
3 egg whites
⅓ cup sugar

Stir together 1 cup sugar and cornstarch in a 2-quart saucepan. Gradually stir in water until smooth. Stir in egg yolks. Stirring constantly, bring to boil over medium heat and boil 1 minute. Remove from heat. Stir in lemon rind, lemon juice and margarine. Cool. Turn into pastry shell. Beat egg whites until foamy in small bowl with mixer at high speed. Add ⅓ cup sugar, 1 Tbs. at a time, beating well after each addition. Continue beating until stiff peaks form. Spread some meringue around edge of filling, first touching crust all around, then fill center. Bake in 350°F. oven 15 minutes, until lightly browned. Cool at room temperature away from draft. Makes 6 to 8 servings.

Key Lime Pie

If recipes were placed in leather-bound books to treasure forever this all-time favorite pie would be included. An inspired Florida genius created this recipe which first appeared on the Eagle Brand Condensed Milk can twenty years ago.

4   eggs, separated
    (reserve 3 whites for
    meringue)
1   can Eagle Brand
    Sweetened Condensed
    Milk
½   cup lime juice
2   to 3 teaspoons grated
    lime rind, optional
    Few drops green food
    coloring

1   8- or 9-inch baked
    pastry shell, cooled
½   tsp. cream of tartar
⅓   cup sugar

Preheat oven to 350°F. In medium bowl, beat egg yolks; stir in sweetened condensed milk, lime juice, rind, and food coloring. In small bowl, stiffly beat 1 egg white; fold into sweetened condensed milk mixture. Turn into shell. Beat reserved egg whites with cream of tartar until foamy; gradually add sugar, beating until stiff but not dry. Spread meringue on top of pie, sealing carefully to edge of shell. Bake 15 minutes or until meringue is golden brown. Cool. Chill before serving. Makes one 8- or 9-inch pie.

Chocolate Butterscotch Pie

America's two favorite flavors, chocolate and butterscotch, combine in this unusual pie recipe from Hershey's famous 1934 cookbook.

¾ cup brown sugar, packed
⅓ cup all-purpose flour
½ tsp. salt
2½ cups milk
6 Tbs. Hershey's Chocolate-Flavored Syrup

2 egg yolks, well beaten
2 Tbs. butter
½ tsp. vanilla
1 9-inch baked pie shell

Thoroughly combine sugar, flour and salt. Stir in milk, chocolate syrup and beaten egg yolks. Cook over medium heat until thick, stirring constantly. Remove from fire; blend in butter and vanilla. Pour into baked pie shell; cool. Chill in refrigerator. Serve with sweetened whipped cream if desired. Makes one 9-inch pie.

Chocolate Pie

Back in 1932 this easy chocolate pie became an instant success and the requests for the recipe are still coming in to the Pet Milk test kitchens.

¾ cup sugar
⅓ cup cornstarch
½ tsp. salt
1 13-ounce can Pet Evaporated Milk
1⅓ cups water
1 Tbs. vanilla

2 squares (1 ounce each) unsweetened chocolate, broken up
1 9-inch frozen Pet-Ritz "Deep Dish" Pie Shell, baked

Mix sugar, cornstarch and salt in large saucepan. Gradually stir in evaporated milk and water. Add chocolate. Cook and stir over medium heat until chocolate is completely melted and mixture boils. Boil 1 minute. Remove from heat. Stir in vanilla. Pour into baked crust. Chill pie at least 2 hours before serving. Serve topped with meringue or Whipped Topping, if desired. Makes one 9-inch pie.

Chocolate Pie With Pretzel Crust

I'll bet you never thought of a pretzel crust, did you? Well, here is one from Rold Gold Pretzels. It's a terrific taste combination and a great change from just plain pie crust.

Crust:
1 13-ounce package Rold Gold Pretzels
3 Tbs. sugar

½ cup butter or margarine, melted

Crush pretzels very fine in blender or between 2 sheets of waxed paper. Add sugar and butter or margarine.

Mix thoroughly. Press half of mixture in 9-inch pie plate. Bake at 350°F. for 8 minutes. Cool. Pour in Chocolate Filling and top with remaining pretzel mixture. Chill. Makes one 9-inch pie.

Chocolate Filling:

⅔ cup sugar
4 Tbs. cornstarch
2½ cups milk
3 1-ounce squares unsweetened chocolate, cut in small pieces

3 egg yolks, slightly beaten
1 tsp. vanilla extract

Combine sugar, cornstarch, milk and chocolate in top of double boiler. Cook over boiling water until thickened, stirring constantly. Cover and cook for 15 minutes. Stir part of hot chocolate mixture into egg yolks. Add to chocolate mixture. Mix thoroughly. Cool. Add vanilla extract and mix thoroughly.

Grasshopper Pie

That Queen of Pies, the Grasshopper. Here's the recipe from the Hiram Walker people just as it appeared in all sorts of advertising a couple of years ago.

Crush 24 chocolate wafer cookies fine, then mix with 3 tablespoons of softened butter and press into a pie plate. Melt 24 marshmallows and ½ cup of milk in the top of a double boiler; after it has cooled, add ¼ cup Hiram Walker Crême de Menthe green and fold in 2 cups of Whipped Cream. Pour into pie shell and chill well. Then, immediately before the pie is served, decorate it with Whipped Cream. Makes one 9-inch pie.

Shoofly Pie

Have you ever baked a Shoofly pie? No? Well this classic from the Grandma's Molasses label is guaranteed to become a favorite at your house. I like it best served warm with a glob of sour cream on top.

1½ cups sifted all-purpose flour
½ cup sugar
⅛ tsp. salt
½ tsp. cinnamon
¼ tsp. ginger
¼ tsp. nutmeg

¼ cup butter or margarine
½ tsp. baking soda
½ cup Grandma's Unsulphured Molasses
¾ cup boiling water
1 unbaked 8-inch pastry shell

Mix together flour, sugar, salt and spices. Cut in butter or margarine until mixture resembles coarse meal. Mix together baking soda and molasses and immediately stir in boiling water. Stir in 1⅓ cups of the crumb mixture. Turn into pastry shell. Sprinkle remaining ⅔ cup of the crumb mixture over top. Bake in 375°F. oven for 30 to 40 minutes, until crust is lightly browned. Serves 6 to 8.

Della Robbia Holiday Pie

The recipe for this beautiful dessert appeared in the Amaretto di Saronno advertising some years ago, and customers still ask for it. The idea is to arrange the leaves and fruit into a "wreath" around the edge of the pie. Truly a spectacular highlight for a holiday buffet table.

1½ cups vanilla wafer crumbs
¼ cup chopped toasted almonds
⅓ cup Amaretto di Saronno liqueur

⅓ cup finely chopped mixed candied fruits
⅓ cup melted butter or margarine
1 quart vanilla ice cream

1 cup heavy cream
2 Tbs. Amaretto di
  Saronno liqueur
1 lb. marzipan fruits or 2
  cups assorted fruits—
  strawberry halves,
  green seedless grapes,
  maraschino cherries,

peach slices, pineapple
chunks, banana slices
or plum slices
Fresh mint leaves or
crystallized mint leaves
(optional)
Candied mimosa and
violets (optional)

In a bowl, mix crumbs, almonds and butter or margarine. Press mixture firmly into an ungreased 9-inch pie pan. Chill. Soften ice cream and stir in ⅓ cup Amaretto di Saronno and fruits. Pour mixture into chilled pie shell. Freeze until hard. In a bowl, mix heavy cream, 2 Tbs. Amaretto di Saronno liqueur; beat until stiff. Pile whipped cream in mounds around the outer edge of pie. Freeze until ready to serve. Decorate pie with marzipan or fruits pressed into whipped cream. Add mint leaves, mimosa and violets if desired. Serve at once. Makes one 9-inch pie.

Never-Fail Pie Crust

Here's a pie crust recipe from Standard Milling Company. Once you have a great pie crust, there is a world of fillings to choose from, a world of pies and quiches you can make.

4 to 4¼ cups Hecker's
  unbleached flour, sifted
1 Tbs. sugar
3 tsps. salt

1 egg
1 Tbs. vinegar
½ cup water
1¾ cups shortening

Sift flour, sugar and salt into a large bowl. Beat the egg and combine with vinegar and water. Cut shortening into flour, sprinkle with egg mixture, and mix all together.

Gather the dough into a ball, wrap in wax paper and chill for about 30 minutes before using.

This dough can be kept in the refrigerator up to 1 week. Or you can divide it into 4 parts (1 pie shell each), wrap each securely and freeze. Makes 4 pie shells or two double crusts.

Jell-O Strawberry Bavarian Pie

A beautiful dessert, gossamer light and smooth as silk. Garnish with whole fresh strawberries if you like.

1 3-ounce package Jell-O Strawberry Gelatin
1 Tbs. sugar
⅛ tsp. salt
1 cup boiling water
½ cup cold water
1 10-ounce package Birds Eye Quick Thaw Strawberries

1 cup Birds Eye Cool Whip Non-Dairy Whipped Topping, thawed
1 baked 9-inch pie shell, cooled

Dissolve Jell-O, sugar and salt in boiling water. Add cold water and frozen strawberries. Stir gently until fruit thaws and separates. Chill until slightly thickened. Add whipped topping; blend until smooth. (Mixture may appear slightly curdled but will smooth out on blending.) Pour into pie shell. Chill until firm, about 4 hours. Garnish with additional whipped topping, and mint leaves, if desired. Makes one 9-inch pie.

Fruit Pies—America's #1 Baked Dessert

From General Foods' kitchens, a handy chart for making the very best fresh fruit pies. Fresh fruit pies thickened with tapioca are bright in taste as well as appearance. Prepare your own two-crust pastry, or make life simple by using a mix. (See directions on Page 122)

Fruit	Prepared fruit	Minute tapioca (Tbs.)	Sugar (cups)	Salt (tsp.)	Flavorings (optional)	Butter or margarine (Tbs.)
Apple*	5 cups (peeled and thinly sliced)	1½	¾	⅛	¾ tsp. cinnamon ¼ tsp. nutmeg	1
Blueberry	4 cups (stemmed)	4	1 to 1¼	¼	⅛ tsp. cinnamon 1½ Tbs. lemon juice	1
Red Sour Cherry	4 cups (pitted)	4	1½	¼	½ tsp. cinnamon ¼ tsp. nutmeg	1
Peach	4 cups (peeled and sliced)	3	¾ to 1	¼	1 Tbs. lemon juice	1
Plum	3 cups (sliced)	3	1	¼	⅛ tsp. cinnamon	1
Rhubarb	4 cups (diced)	3	1½	¼	1 tsp. grated orange rind	1
Strawberry	4 cups (hulled)	3	½	¼	1 tsp. lemon juice	None

* Use Greening, Cortland, Rome Beauty, Wealthy or McIntosh.

Directions for using chart (page 121)

Combine all ingredients except butter. Let stand about 15 minutes. Pour into pastry-lined 9-inch pie pan. Dot with butter. Add top crust. Seal and flute edge. Cut and open slits in top crust to permit escape of steam. Bake at 425°F. until syrup boils with heavy bubbles that do not burst, 45 to 55 minutes. Cool before cutting.

7.
Prize-
Winning
Cakes

If it's a festive occasion, it's time for a cake! The very word sounds special: wedding cake, birthday cake, Christmas cake—all great and wonderful days call for nothing less than a beautiful, big, homemade cake.

Way back in the Forties there was an immensely popular, if silly, song, "If I'd Known You Were Coming, I'd Have Baked a Cake." It was fun, and it did put into words that special something about a homemade cake. Despite all this, a lot of people put off cake making. Why? I suspect because they think of cake making as troublesome and not a few are haunted by late-lamented failures. Well, put all that behind you. Cake making is fun when the experts have worked out recipes that are super-easy and super-sure of success. You can rest assured that *every* recipe in this chapter has been perfected to the point where it simply can't fail.

And what recipes! Deep, dark, rich devil's food; airy angel cake; a butterscotch chiffon cake, creamy textured with an all-time favorite butterscotch flavor; and there are $25,000 prize-winning cakes from the Pillsbury Bake Off, and cakes that made Bacardi Rum household words; plus frostings, fillings and glazes to crown each success with new laurels—from dependable old-fashioned seven-minute frosting to a rich rum filling. Last but not least, an authentic Linzer Torte.

Wouldn't it be fun to surprise your family with a luscious, big cake tonight? As for parties, there's no more beautiful sight on a buffet table than a perfect cake, and, may I let you in on a very special party secret? A famous hostess, known for her fabulous parties down in Dallas, Texas, where the sky's the limit when it comes to parties, never fails to have a luscious devil's food cake and a pot of always hot coffee on a side table when she gives one of her justly celebrated cocktail buffets. It seems her guests love this combination as the best "one for the road" ever.

Now if I had known you were coming I would have baked you a cake—in fact I will anyway. Maybe you will drop in this afternoon and it pays to be ready.

Devil's Food Cake

For the thousands of people who thought they had lost it forever, here's that great Devil's Food cake recipe from the Swans Down Cake Flour box. It's the *best* devil's food cake that ever was. I've made it for thirty years.

2½ cups sifted Swans Down
    Cake Flour
1¾ cups sugar
1¾ tsps. baking soda
1 tsp. salt
⅔ cup shortening (at
    room temperature)

1⅓ cups milk
1 tsp. vanilla
2 eggs
3 squares Baker's
    Unsweetened
    Chocolate, melted and
    cooled

Sift flour with sugar, soda, and salt. Stir shortening to soften. Add flour mixture, 1 cup milk, and vanilla; mix until flour is dampened. Then beat 2 minutes at medium speed of electric mixer or 300 vigorous strokes by hand. Add eggs, melted chocolate and remaining ⅓ cup milk; beat 1 minute longer with mixer or 150 strokes by hand. Pour into two greased and floured 9-inch layer pans. Bake at 350°F. about 35 minutes, until cake tester inserted in center comes out clean. Cool 10 minutes in pans; remove from pans and cool thoroughly on racks.

Alternate baking pans: This cake may also be baked at 350°F. in three 8-inch layer pans about 30 minutes or in a 13 × 9-inch pan about 40 minutes. Recipe may be doubled, if desired. If necessary, refrigerate part of the batter while first layers bake.

Seven-Minute Frosting

And here's the perfect icing for devil's food or almost any cake. Peaks of this snowy white frosting crown a cake in regal fashion.

2 egg whites	⅓ cup water
1½ cups sugar	2 tsps. light corn syrup
Dash of salt	1 tsp. vanilla

Combine egg whites, sugar, salt, water, and corn syrup in top of double boiler. Beat 1 minute or until thoroughly mixed. Then place over boiling water and beat constantly at high speed of electric mixer or with rotary beater for 7 minutes, until frosting will stand in stiff peaks; stir frosting up from bottom and sides of pan occasionally. Remove from boiling water and pour at once into a large bowl. Add vanilla and beat 1 minute, until thick enough to spread. Makes about 4½ cups, enough to cover tops and sides of two 8- or 9-inch layers or a 10-inch tube cake.

Variation: For your Devil's Food Cake, you might like to try . . .

Vanilla "Philly" Frosting

We couldn't go to press without this all-time classic recipe for frosting. Kraft tells us over two million good cooks have asked for the recipe since it was offered on an early Kraft television show. Thousands of plaintive cries to replace "the one I saved from the Philadelphia Cream Cheese package" come in to the Kraft kitchens each year.

1 8-ounce package
Philadelphia Brand
Cream Cheese
1 Tbs. milk

1 tsp. vanilla
Dash of salt
5½ cups sifted
confectioners' sugar

Blend together softened cream cheese, milk, vanilla and salt. Add sugar, 1 cup at a time, mixing well after each addition. Fills and frosts two 8- or 9-inch cake layers.

Variations:
Substitute 1 tsp. almond extract for vanilla.
Stir in ¼ cup crushed peppermint candy.
Stir in ¼ cup crushed lemon drops and 1 tsp. lemon juice.

German Sweet Chocolate Cake

In 1958 this all-time favorite cake appeared on Baker's Sweet Chocolate package. As the years passed, its popularity grew. Today it's one of the most requested recipes of the General Foods' kitchens.

1 4-ounce package
Baker's German Sweet
Chocolate
½ cup boiling water
2½ cups sifted Swans Down
Cake Flour*
1 tsp. baking soda
½ tsp. salt

1 cup butter or
margarine
2 cups sugar
4 egg yolks
1 tsp. vanilla
1 cup buttermilk
4 egg whites
Coconut-Pecan Filling
and Frosting

Melt chocolate in boiling water; cool. Sift flour with soda and salt. Cream butter and sugar until light and fluffy.

* Or use 2¼ cups sifted all-purpose flour.

Add egg yolks, one at a time, beating after each addition. Blend in vanilla and melted chocolate. Add flour mixture, alternately with the buttermilk, beating after each addition until smooth. Beat egg whites until they form stiff peaks; fold into batter. Pour batter into three 9-inch layer pans which have been lined on bottoms with paper. Bake at 350°F. for 30 to 35 minutes, until cake springs back when lightly pressed in center. Cool cake in pans 15 minutes; then remove and cool on rack. Spread Coconut-Pecan Filling and Frosting between layers and over top of cake.

Note: This delicate cake will have a flat slightly sugary top crust which tends to crack.

Coconut-Pecan Filling and Frosting

1 cup evaporated milk or heavy cream
1 cup sugar
3 egg yolks, slightly beaten
½ cup butter or margarine

1 tsp. vanilla
1⅓ cups (about) Baker's Angel Flake or Premium Shred Coconut
1 cup chopped pecans

Combine milk, sugar, egg yolks, butter and vanilla in a saucepan. Cook over medium heat, stirring constantly until mixture thickens, about 12 minutes. Remove from heat. Add coconut and pecans. Cool until of spreading consistency, beating occasionally.

Makes 2½ cups or enough to cover tops of three 9-inch layers.

Note: For thinner frosting, use only 2 egg yolks.

Hershey's Red Velvet Cocoa Cake

In the Thirties money was scarce and luxuries were few. No wonder this economy-minded cake recipe from Hershey's Cocoa was a favorite then. It still is! Moist and rich tasting, it calls for only ½ cup of shortening and two eggs, but it tastes as extravagant as any cake you've ever made.

½ cup shortening	2½ cups sifted cake flour
1½ cups sugar	1 cup buttermilk
2 eggs	1 tsp. salt
1 tsp. vanilla	1 tsp. soda
3 Tbs. Hershey's Cocoa	1 Tbs. vinegar
2 ounces red food coloring	

Cream shortening and sugar. Add eggs and vanilla. Beat well. In a separate dish, blend cocoa and food coloring; add to sugar mixture. Add flour, buttermilk, and salt alternately. Mix soda and vinegar in cup and add.

Bake in two 9-inch cake pans, greased and floured, at 350°F. for 30 to 35 minutes. If desired, divide batter between three 8-inch pans. Let cool before frosting.

Note: A red paste coloring usually does a prettier job than some liquid types. They are available in specialty shops or in cake decorating supply sections of department stores.

Lovelight Chiffon Yellow Cake

Here's that famous all-time favorite cake from Wesson Oil.

2 eggs, separated
1½ cups sugar
2¼ cups sifted cake flour
3 tsps. baking powder

1 tsp. salt
⅓ cup Wesson Oil
1 cup milk
1½ tsps. vanilla

Heat oven to 350°F. Lightly oil and dust with flour two round 8- or 9-inch layer pans. Beat egg whites until frothy. Gradually beat in ½ cup of sugar. Continue beating until very stiff and glossy. Sift remaining sugar, flour, baking powder and salt into another bowl. Add Wesson Oil, half the milk, and vanilla. Beat 1 minute, medium speed on the mixer, or 150 strokes by hand. Scrape sides and bottom of bowl constantly. Add remaining milk, and egg yolks, then beat 1 minute more, scraping the sides of the bowl constantly. Fold in meringue. Pour into prepared pans. Bake layers for 30 to 35 minutes. Cool then frost with Seven-Minute Frosting (see page 126).

Chocolate Mayonnaise Cake

Mayonnaise in a cake? Yes, and what's more, thousands of cooks have written in for copies of this old favorite printed on the Hellmann's jar.

2 cups unsifted flour
⅔ cup unsweetened cocoa
1¼ tsps. baking soda
¼ tsp. baking powder
1⅔ cups sugar

3 eggs
1 tsp. vanilla
1 cup Hellmann's or Best Foods Real Mayonnaise
1⅓ cups water

Grease and flour bottoms of two 9 × 1½-inch round baking pans. In medium bowl stir together flour, cocoa, baking soda and baking powder; set aside. In large bowl with mixer at high speed beat sugar, eggs and vanilla, occasionally scraping bowl, 3 minutes or until light and fluffy. Reduce speed to low; beat in mayonnaise. Add flour mixture in 4 additions alternately with water, beginning and ending with flour. Pour into prepared pans. Bake in 350°F. oven for 30 to 35 minutes or until cake tester inserted in center comes out clean. Cool in pans for 10 minutes. Remove; cool on wire racks. Frost as desired. Garnish with sliced almonds. Makes two 9-inch layers.

Angel Food Cake

Did you think I would leave this one out? It's a classic from Swans Down.

1¼ cups sifted Swans Down
    Cake Flour
½ cup sugar
1½ cups (about 12) egg
    whites (at room
    temperature)
¼ tsp. salt

1¼ tsps. cream of tartar
1 tsp. vanilla
¼ tsp. almond extract
1⅓ cups sugar
    Butter Cream Frosting
    or Sweet Chocolate
    Glaze

Sift flour with ½ cup sugar four times. Combine egg whites, salt, cream of tartar and flavorings in large bowl. Beat with a flat wire whip, rotary beater or high speed of electric mixer until moist, glossy; soft peaks will form. Add 1⅓ cups sugar, sprinkling in ⅓ cup at a time and beating until blended after each addition, about 25 strokes by hand. Sift in flour mixture in four additions, folding in with 15 complete fold-over strokes after each addition and turning bowl often. After last addition, use 10 to 20 extra strokes. Pour into an ungreased 10-inch tube pan. Bake at 375°F. for 35 to 40 minutes, or until the top springs back when pressed lightly. Invert on rack and cool thoroughly. Then remove from pan and frost.

Butter Cream Frosting

Fluffier than most, this butter frosting adds to your cake's elegance.

½ cup butter or margarine
⅛ tsp. salt
1 lb. unsifted
    confectioners' sugar

1 egg or 2 egg yolks
1 tsp. vanilla
2 Tbs. (about) milk

Cream butter and salt; gradually add part of the sugar, blending well after each addition. Stir in egg and vanilla. Add remaining sugar alternately with milk, until of spreading consistency, beating after each addition until smooth. Makes 2½ cups, or enough to cover tops and sides of two 9-inch layers, three 8-inch layers, a 9-inch square, a 13 × 9-inch cake, or a 10-inch tube cake.

Coffee Butter Cream Frosting. Prepare as for Butter Cream Frosting, adding 1 Tbs. Instant Maxwell House, Sanka, or Yuban Coffee and decreasing the vanilla to ½ tsp.

Sweet Chocolate Glaze

Just enough dark, glossy glaze to crown a cake beautifully, deliciously.

1 4-ounce package
Baker's German Sweet
Chocolate
1 Tbs. butter
3 Tbs. water

1 cup sifted confectioners'
sugar
Dash of salt
½ tsp. vanilla

Combine chocolate, butter and water in a small saucepan; stir over low heat until blended and smooth. Combine sugar and salt in mixing bowl. Gradually add chocolate mixture, blending well. Add vanilla. (For thinner glaze, stir in a little hot water; for thicker glaze, cool mixture until of desired consistency). Makes ¾ cup, or enough to glaze top of a 9- or 10-inch tube cake, 8- or 9-inch layer, or 13 × 9-inch cake.

Fantasy Sponge Cake

Swans Down's traditional six-egg cake—a good basis for hundreds of desserts.

6 egg whites (¾ cup),
room temperature
1 tsp. cream of tartar
1½ cups sifted sugar
1⅓ cups sifted Swans Down
Cake Flour

½ tsp. Calumet Baking
Powder
½ tsp. salt
6 egg yolks (½ cup)
¼ cup water
1 tsp. lemon extract

Beat egg whites with cream of tartar in a large bowl until soft mounds begin to form, using high speed of electric mixer or rotary beater or flat wire whip. Beat in ½ cup of sugar, 2 Tbs. at a time; then beat until very stiff peaks form; do not underbeat. Sift flour with remaining 1 cup sugar, baking powder and salt into a small bowl. Add egg yolks, water and lemon extract; beat with a spoon just until blended (about 75 strokes). Carefully fold into egg white mixture, using about 30 fold-over strokes; do not stir or beat. Pour into an ungreased 10-inch tube pan; gently cut through batter to remove large air bubbles. Bake at 375°F. for about 35 minutes, until cake springs back when pressed lightly. Invert and cool thoroughly in pan. Remove from pan; sprinkle with sifted confectioners' sugar or top with a glaze, if desired. Makes one 10-inch tube cake.

Spicy Butterscotch Chiffon Cake

Here is a recipe for an unusual Butterscotch Chiffon Cake that appeared on the Domino Sugar carton a few years ago. It's a delightfully different cake, light and spicy. I like it best with Seven-Minute Frosting (see page 126).

2¼ cups sifted cake flour	½ cup salad oil
3 tsps. double-acting baking powder	5 egg yolks
1 tsp. salt	¾ cup water
½ tsp. each allspice, cinnamon, cloves and nutmeg	2 tsps. vanilla
	1 cup egg whites, room temperature
2 cups Domino Light Brown Sugar	½ tsp. cream of tartar

Sift together flour, baking powder, salt and spices in large mixing bowl. Stir sugar into mixture. Make a well in dry ingredients; add oil, yolks, water and extract. Beat thoroughly until sugar is dissolved and batter is smooth.

Place egg whites in large mixing bowl. Sprinkle cream of tartar on whites. Beat at highest speed until whites stand in peaks but are not dry. Gradually fold batter into beaten egg whites, turning mixture over lightly from bottom with rubber spatula until well blended. Do not stir or overmix.

Turn into ungreased 10-inch tube pan. Bake in slow 325°F oven. for 80 to 85 minutes until cake springs back when touched lightly. Invert pan on funnel or suspend over cooling rack. Allow cake to hang until cool. Remove by running a sharp thin-bladed knife around sides of pan with one long steady stroke. Tap pan sharply until cake comes free. Makes one 10-inch cake.

Happy Day Cake

This is an all-time favorite from the Swans Down Cake Flour package.

2½ cups sifted Swans Down
　　Cake Flour
1½ cups sugar
　3 tsps. Calumet Baking
　　Powder
　1 tsp. salt

½ cup shortening (at
　　room temperature)
1 cup milk
1 tsp. vanilla
2 eggs

Sift flour with sugar, baking powder, and salt. Stir shortening to soften. Add flour mixture, ¾ cup of the milk, and vanilla. Mix until all flour is dampened; then beat 2 minutes at medium speed of electric mixer or 300 vigorous strokes by hand. Add eggs and remaining ¼ cup milk; beat 1 minute longer with mixer or 150 strokes by hand. Pour into two 9-inch layer pans that have been lined on bottoms with paper. Bake at 350°F. for 25 to 30 minutes, or until cake tester inserted in center comes out clean. Cool 10 minutes in pans; remove from pans and cool thoroughly on racks. Frost with any favorite frosting.

Alternate baking pans: This cake may also be baked

at 350°F. in three 8-inch layer pans for 25 to 35 minutes, or in a 13 × 9-inch pan for 30 to 35 minutes. Or spoon the batter into 36 medium paper baking cups in muffin pans, filling each half full; then bake at 375°F. for 20 to 25 minutes.

Coconut Praline Cake: Prepare as for Happy Day Cake, adding ⅔ cup Baker's Angel Flake Coconut with the eggs; bake in 13 × 9-inch pan as directed. Meanwhile, prepare Coconut Praline Topping. Spread topping over hot cake in pan; broil until bubbly and golden brown.

Coconut Praline Topping

A broiled-on topping that's delicious hot or cool.

Melt ½ cup butter; then add 1 cup firmly packed brown sugar, 1⅓ cups (about) Baker's Angel Flake Coconut, and ⅓ cup light cream, mixing well. Let stand about 5 minutes. Then spread mixture over top of either warm or cold cake. Broil until topping is bubbly and golden brown, about 3 minutes. Serve warm or cold. Makes about 1⅔ cups, or enough to cover top of a 13 × 9-inch cake or a 10-inch tube cake.

Plum Good Cake

Ever think of using baby food to make a cake? The Gerber people did and printed this recipe on their strained plum jars years ago. It's a lovely, moist, rich cake and a snap to make.

2 cups unsifted flour	½ tsp. baking powder
2 cups granulated sugar	½ tsp. baking soda
½ tsp. salt	1 tsp. cinnamon

½ tsp. cloves
1 cup salad oil
3 eggs
2 jars (4¾ ounces each) Gerber Strained Plums with Tapioca

1 Tbs. red food coloring
1 cup chopped black walnuts or other nuts (optional)

Mix all ingredients at one time with electric beater until eggs are well mixed. Pour into greased Bundt or tube cake pan. Bake in preheated 300°F. oven for 1 hour and 10 minutes or until sides of cake pull away from pan. Remove cake from pan while still hot. Frost while hot.

Frosting: 1 cup confectioners sugar combined with 1 Tbs. lemon juice (will be quite thick). Let cool before serving.

Nutty Graham Picnic Cake

A Pillsbury Bake-Off winner! A brown sugar glaze topped with nuts adds just the right finish to this moist, hearty cake.

2 cups Pillsbury's Best All Purpose or Unbleached Flour*
1 cup (14 squares) graham craker crumbs
1 cup firmly packed brown sugar
½ cup sugar
1 tsp. salt

1 tsp. baking powder
1 tsp. baking soda
½ tsp. cinnamon
1 cup margarine or butter, softened
1 cup orange juice
1 Tbs. grated orange peel
3 eggs
1 cup chopped nuts

Glaze:

2 Tbs. brown sugar
5 tsps. milk
1 Tbs. margarine or butter

¾ cup powdered sugar
¼ cup chopped nuts

* If you use Pillsbury's Best Self-Rising Flour, omit salt and baking powder and reduce soda to ¼ tsp.

Heat oven to 350°F. Using 1 Tbs. solid shortening, generously grease and flour 12-cup fluted tube pan or 10-inch tube pan (non-stick finish). Lightly spoon flour into measuring cup; level off. In large bowl, combine all cake ingredients except nuts; beat 3 minutes at medium speed. Stir in nuts. Pour into prepared pan. Bake at 350°F. for 45 to 50 minutes or until toothpick inserted in center comes out clean. Cool upright in pan for 15 minutes; invert onto serving plate, cool completely.

Glaze: In small saucepan, heat 2 Tbs. brown sugar, milk and butter just until melted. Remove from heat; add powdered sugar and blend until smooth. Drizzle over cake; sprinkle with nuts. Makes 12 to 16 servings.

High Altitude: Above 3500 feet, bake at 350°F. for 50 to 55 minutes.

Bacardi Rum Cake

Here's the very first cake to incorporate a pudding mix. It's simply fabulous.

Cake:
- 1 cup chopped pecans or walnuts
- 1 18½-ounce package yellow cake mix
- 1 3¾-ounce package Jell-O Instant Vanilla Pudding mix
- 4 eggs
- ¼ cup cold water
- ½ cup Wesson oil
- ½ cup Bacardi Dark Rum (80 proof)

Glaze:
- ¼ lb. butter
- ¼ cup water
- 1 cup granulated sugar
- ½ cup Bacardi Dark Rum (80 proof)

Preheat oven to 325°F. Grease and flour 10-inch tube or 12-cup Bundt pan. Sprinkle nuts over bottom of pan. Mix all cake ingredients together. Pour batter over nuts. Bake 1 hour. Cool. Invert on serving plate. Prick top. Drizzle and smooth glaze evenly over top and sides. Allow cake to absorb glaze. Repeat till all glaze is used up.

Glaze: Melt butter in saucepan. Stir in water and sugar. Boil 5 minutes, stirring constantly. Remove from heat. Stir in rum.

Optional: Decorate with whole maraschino cherries and border of sugar frosting or whipped cream. Serve with seedless green grapes dusted with powdered sugar.

Orange Kiss-Me Cake

This cake is still as good as it was in 1950 when it was named the $25,000 Pillsbury Bake-Off winner. The delicious flavor comes from a fresh orange, raisins and walnuts ground together. Modern methods make it so easy to prepare that you can enjoy this cake often. A blender or food processor makes short work of grinding the fruit and nuts.

2 cups Pillsbury's Best All Purpose or Unbleached Flour
1 orange
1 cup raisins
⅓ cup walnuts

1 cup sugar
1 tsp. baking soda
1 tsp. salt
1 cup milk
½ cup shortening
2 eggs

Topping:

Reserved ⅓ cup orange juice
⅓ cup sugar
1 tsp. cinnamon

¼ cup finely chopped walnuts
Orange slices, to garnish

Heat oven to 350°F. (325°F. for glass pan). Grease (not oil) and flour 13 × 9-inch pan. Lightly spoon flour into measuring cup; level off. Squeeze orange; reserve ⅓ cup juice. Grind orange peel and pulp, raisins and ⅓ cup walnuts together. Set aside. In large bowl, blend flour, sugar, soda, salt, milk, shortening and eggs. Beat for 3 minutes at medium speed. Stir in orange-raisin mixture. Pour into prepared pan.

Bake at 350°F. for 35 to 40 minutes or until toothpick inserted in center comes out clean.

Topping: Drizzle reserved orange juice over warm cake. Combine sugar, cinnamon and walnuts; sprinkle over cake. If desired, garnish with orange slices. Makes a 13 × 9-inch cake.

Notes: Self-rising flour not recommended. A blender may be used to grind orange-raisin mixture if grinder is unavailable. This has not been tested in a food processor, but it should work.

High Altitude: Above 3500 feet, add 2 Tbs. flour; bake at 375°F. for 35 to 40 minutes.

Bacardi Rum Piña Colada Cake

Can you believe it? It's even better than the original rum cake—if that's possible!

Cake:

1 package (2-layer size) white cake mix	4 eggs
	¼ cup water*
1 package (4-serving size) Jell-O Coconut Cream Flavor or Vanilla Instant Pudding and Pie Filling*	⅓ cup Bacardi Dark Rum (80 proof)
	¼ cup Wesson oil
	1 cup flaked coconut

* With vanilla flavor filling, increase water to ¾ cup; add 1 cup flaked coconut to batter.

Frosting:

1 8-ounce can crushed
  pineapple (in juice)
1 package (4-serving size)
  Jell-O Coconut Cream
  Flavor or Vanilla Instant
  Pudding and Pie Filling

⅓ cup Bacardi Dark Rum
  (80 proof)
1 9-ounce container frozen
  whipped topping,
  thawed

Blend all ingredients except coconut in large mixer bowl. Beat 4 minutes at medium speed of electric mixer. Pour into two greased and floured 9-inch layer pans. Bake at 350°F. for 25 to 30 minutes or until cake springs back when lightly pressed. Do not underbake. Cool in pan for 15 minutes; remove and cool on racks. Fill and frost; sprinkle with coconut. Chill. Refrigerate leftover cake.

Frosting: Combine all ingredients except whipped topping in a bowl; beat until well blended. Fold in thawed whipped topping.

Dream Cake

The idea of adding to a cake mix isn't so new after all. In 1969 General Foods developed this recipe for a luscious, creamy cake that uses a packet of Dream Whip for its velvety taste and texture.

1 package (2-layer size)
  yellow, white or devil's
  food cake mix
1 envelope Dream Whip
  Whipped Topping Mix*

4 eggs
1 cup cold water

Combine cake mix, whipped topping mix right from envelope, eggs and water in large bowl of electric

* Do not whip; use right from envelope.

mixer. Blend until moistened. Beat at medium speed for 4 minutes. Pour into greased and floured 10-inch tube pan. Bake at 350°F. for 45 to 50 minutes or until cake tester inserted into center of cake comes out clean. Cool in pan 15 minutes. Then loosen from sides and center tube with knife and gently remove cake. Finish cooling on rack.

Note: Reduce temperature to 325°F. when using glass baking dishes.

Alternate baking pans: This cake may also be baked in the following greased and floured pans, cooling in pans 10 minutes:

Two 9-inch layer pans for 30 minutes.

Two 8-inch square pans for about 30 minutes.

Three 8-inch layer pans for about 35 minutes.

Three 8 × 3½-inch aluminum loaf pans for 30 to 40 minutes.

Two 9 × 5-inch loaf pans for 45 minutes.

One 13 × 9-inch pan for 40 to 45 minutes.

Two 15 × 10-inch jelly roll pans for 12 to 14 minutes.

40 medium cupcake pans (one-half to two-thirds full) for 20 minutes.

One 10-inch Bundt pan for 40 minutes; cool in pan for 15 minutes.

Three 8 × 4-inch loaf pans for 30 to 40 minutes.

Tomato Spice Cake

A half century of good cooks have baked this Campbell's Tomato Soup cake. It's as moist, delicate and delicious today as it was fifty years ago.

2¼ cups cake flour or 2 cups all-purpose flour

1⅓ cups sugar
4 tsps. baking powder

1 tsp. baking soda
1½ tsps. allspice
1 tsp. cinnamon
½ tsp. ground cloves
1 10¾-ounce can
   Campbell's Condensed
   Tomato Soup

½ cup shortening
2 eggs
¼ cup water

Preheat oven to 350°F. Generously grease and flour two round 8- or 9-inch layer pans, or a 13 × 9 × 2-inch oblong pan. Measure dry ingredients into large bowl. Add soup and shortening. Beat at low to medium speed for 2 minutes or 300 strokes with a spoon, scraping sides and bottom of bowl constantly. Add eggs and water. Beat 2 minutes more, scraping bowl frequently. Pour into pans. Bake for 35 to 40 minutes. Let stand 10 minutes; remove. Cool. Use Vanilla Philly Frosting (page 126).

Bundt pan: Proceed as above. Bake in well-greased and lightly floured 2½-quart Bundt pan at 350°F. for 50 to 60 minutes or until done. Cool right-side-up in pan for 15 minutes; remove from pan. Cool. If desired, sprinkle with confectioners' sugar.

It's-A-Snap Cheesecake

The Knox Gelatine people printed this sure-fire recipe for cheesecake on their package years ago. It's become a classic, so don't hesitate. Make it for dessert the next time you want to serve something impressive.

1 envelope Knox
   Unflavored Gelatine
½ cup sugar
1 cup boiling water

2 8-ounce packages
   cream cheese, softened
1 tsp. vanilla (optional)
1 9-inch graham cracker
   crust

In a large bowl, mix Knox Unflavored Gelatine and sugar; add boiling water and stir until gelatine is completely dissolved. With electric mixer, beat in cream cheese and vanilla until smooth. Pour into prepared crust; chill until firm, about 2 hours. Top, if desired, with fresh or canned fruit. Makes about 8 servings.

For delicious variations try:

Marbled Cheesecake: Before chilling, marble in ⅓ cup chocolate fudge, butterscotch or your favorite flavor ice cream topping.

Lemon or Almond Cheesecake: Substitute ½ to ¾ teaspoon lemon or almond extract for vanilla extract.

Fruit 'n Creamy Cheesecake: Chill cheesecake for 10 minutes, then swirl in ⅓ cup strawberry or raspberry preserves.

Sunshine Cheesecake: Substitute ½ teaspoon orange extract for vanilla extract and add 1 teaspoon grated orange rind.

Bacardi Rum Chocolate Cake

And now there's a chocolate version to split and fill with a heady chocolate filling.

1 18½-ounce package chocolate cake mix

1 package (4-serving size) Jell-O Chocolate Instant Pudding and Pie Filling

4 eggs

½ cup Bacardi Dark Rum (80 proof)

¼ cup cold water

½ cup Wesson oil

½ cup slivered almonds, optional

Filling:

1½ cups cold milk
¼ cup Bacardi Dark Rum (80 proof)
1 package (4-serving size) Jell-O Chocolate
Instant Pudding and Pie Filling
1 envelope Dream Whip Topping Mix

Preheat oven to 350°F. Grease and flour two 9-inch layer cake pans. Combine all cake ingredients together in large bowl. Blend well, then beat at medium mixer speed for 2 minutes. Turn into prepared pans. Bake for 30 minutes or until cake tests done. Do not underbake. Cool in pans for 10 minutes. Remove from pans, finish cooling on racks. Split layers in half horizontally. Spread 1 cup filling between each layer and over top of cake. Stack. Keep cake chilled. Serve cold.

Optional: Garnish with chocolate curls.

Filling: Combine milk, rum, pudding mix and topping mix in deep narrow-bottom bowl. Blend well at high speed for 4 minutes, until light and fluffy. Makes 4 cups.

Goodie Apple Sauce Cake

The Stokely Company printed this recipe on its apple sauce label. It's cake that stays fresh for days!

2½ cups all-purpose flour
1 cup sugar
¼ tsp. baking powder
1½ tsps. baking soda
1½ tsps. salt
¾ tsp. cinnamon
½ tsp. cloves, ground
½ tsp. allspice
½ cup shortening, softened
½ cup water
½ cup nut meats, broken
1 cup raisins, cut up
1 1-lb. can Stokely's Finest Gravenstein Apple Sauce
1 large egg

Sift together first eight ingredients. Add next four ingredients and beat for 2 minutes. Add last two ingredients and beat 2 more minutes. Pour into greased and floured 12 × 7½-inch pan and bake at 350°F. for 45 to 50 minutes. Top with your favorite lemon frosting. Makes 18 servings.

Note: For best flavor, bake the day before serving.

Linzer Torte

A dozen years ago Blue Diamond Almonds introduced this scrumptious and authentic Linzer Torte. Serve it with clouds of real whipped cream in true Viennese fashion and don't forget the coffee.

1½ cups Blue Diamond Whole Natural Almonds
1 cup butter or margarine
1 cup sugar
2 egg yolks, beaten
1½ tsps. grated lemon rind
2 cups sifted all-purpose flour
1 Tbs. cinnamon
½ tsp. ground cloves
1 cup raspberry jam

Grind almonds in blender or food processor; set aside. Cream butter and sugar. Add egg yolks, ground almonds and lemon rind. Sift together flour and spices and add to creamed mixture. Knead until dough is firm and holds together. Pat two-thirds of dough into a 9-inch round cake pan, covering bottom and sides. The layer should be about ½ inch thick. Spread with jam. Form eight ½-inch thick strips with remaining dough. Make lattice top by placing four strips one way and 4 the opposite. Bake in 350°F. oven for 30 to 40 minutes. Cool. Cut into pie-shaped wedges 1 inch wide at the rim. Makes about 30 pieces.

8.
A Variety
of
Desserts

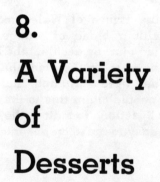

Desserts are "soul food," the crown of the meal, the sweet ending which, "like in the movies," everybody wants. In fact, there is something unfinished about a meal without dessert.

So here we give you a collection to satisfy your soul, to end on a sweet note that leaves everyone happy. Some of them have been pleasing people for half a century, some are new; all are as easy as smiling and every one tastes scrumptious. These are professional recipes, created by true professionals. You can be sure of perfect results each and every time you decide to make each and every recipe.

Cointreau Crêpes

One day the Prince of Wales requested a thin French pancake with a blend of orange and lemon peel and Cointreau Liqueur. By accident the liqueur caught fire, and with no time to re-do the dish, the pancakes were served flaming. They were a triumph, and the rest is history. The Cointreau people claim this is the true story of the origin of "Crêpes Suzette." No matter, the sauce is lovely and will turn these easy-to-make crêpes into a truly festive dessert.

Crêpes:

2 eggs	2 Tbs. melted butter
2 egg yolks	¾ cup flour
1 cup milk	1 Tbs. sugar
1 Tbs. Cointreau Liqueur	½ tsp. salt

Beat to combine eggs, egg yolks, milk, Cointreau and melted butter. Stir in dry ingredients until smooth. Heat 6- or 7-inch skillet; brush with butter. Pour in 2 Tbs. batter, tilting pan to spread. Brown both sides. Repeat with rest of batter. Makes about 16 crêpes.

Cointreau Crêpe Sauce: Prepare one dozen dessert crêpes and fold into triangles. In a chafing dish, heat 1 stick butter, 8 sugar cubes, ½ teaspoon grated orange rind (or more to taste) and the juice of 1 orange. Cook, stirring until smooth. Turn crêpes in this mixture and arrange neatly in pan. Pour over ½ cup Cointreau Liqueur, basting crêpes until flames subside. Serves 4.

Crêpes L'Ananas Deluxe

Straight from a deluxe restaurant, voilà! Very special crêpes dreamed up by Dole Pineapple for your next party.

1 can (1 lb., 4 ounces) Dole Crushed Pineapple in Juice	⅛ tsp. salt
	2 Tbs. unflavored gelatine
2 egg yolks, slightly beaten	1½ cups cottage cheese
½ cup sugar	1½ tsps. vanilla
1 tsp. grated lemon peel	1 cup whipped cream
	5 to 6 Dessert Crêpes

Drain pineapple, reserving all juice. Set aside 2 Tbs. pineapple for garnish. Combine egg yolks, sugar, lemon peel, salt and 1 Tbs. pineapple juice in a double boiler. Cook over medium heat, stirring continuously until mixture is smooth and thickened, about 5 minutes. Remove from heat. Soften gelatine in remaining pineapple juice; add to cooked mixture, stirring until thoroughly dissolved. Blend in crushed pineapple, cottage cheese and vanilla. Cool slightly. Reserve ¼ cup whipped cream for garnish. Fold balance of whipped cream into pineapple mixture. Chill. Place one crêpe on a pedestal cake plate or other serving dish. Spread 1 cup pineapple mixture evenly over crêpe. Top with second crêpe. Repeat until crêpe stack is 4 to 5 layers high. Top with reserved ¼ cup whipped cream and 2 Tbs. crushed pineapple in center. Chill before serving. Makes 4 to 6 servings.

Note: For extra ease in cutting, freeze dessert for 40 minutes before serving. Use a long, sharp knife to cut.

Dessert Crêpes

3 eggs	½ cup flour
½ cup milk	1 tsp. sugar
2 Tbs. butter, melted	Dash salt

Combine all ingredients and blend well. Refrigerate for at least 1 hour. Lightly oil a 6-inch crêpe pan. Set pan over medium heat. Pour ⅛ cup crêpe batter into pan. Tilt and swirl batter to coat pan evenly. Cook until edges darken slightly. Lift with spatula and cook on other side. Lift onto a sheet of wax paper. Continue with remaining batter. Stack crêpes with a sheet of wax paper separating each. Store in refrigerator or freezer.

Note: If you use an electric crêpe machine, prepare crêpes according to manufacturer's instructions.

Chocolate-Marshmallow Cream Roll

A simply beautiful and extra-festive dessert. A sensation ever since it appeared in a 1930s Hershey advertisement.

6 egg yolks	½ cup cake flour
6 Tbs. Hershey's Cocoa	1 tsp. vanilla
1 heaping cup 4X sugar (confectioners')	6 egg whites, stiffly beaten
Dash of salt	

Beat egg yolks until thick and lemon-colored; add cocoa, sugar, salt, flour and vanilla (mixture will be stiff). Fold in one-fourth of the stiffly beaten egg whites; blend well. Fold in remaining egg whites; turn into a greased 15 × 9 × 2-inch pan lined with waxed paper. Bake in a 350°F. oven 20 minutes. Turn out onto a damp towel, roll up and let rest 1 minute. Unroll and reroll without towel. Cool on rack covered with waxed paper. Fill with Marshmallow Peppermint Icing and cover with half recipe Bitter Chocolate Butter Icing. If desired, garnish with flowers made by cutting marshmallows into very thin strips, using candied cherries as centers. Makes 12 servings.

Marshmallow Peppermint Icing

2 Tbs. water
½ cup granulated sugar
1 egg white, beaten stiff
¾ cup marshmallow whip

¼ tsp. peppermint extract
Few drops red food coloring
Few grains salt

Boil water and sugar together until the soft ball stage is reached (234°F.). Slowly pour hot syrup over beaten egg white, beating constantly. Add marshmallow whip, salt, extract and food coloring; beat until cool. Makes 2¼ cups icing or enough for a 13 × 9 × 2-inch loaf cake.

Bitter Chocolate Butter Icing

½ cup butter
2 cups 4X sugar
  (confectioners')

2 Tbs. light cream
4 squares Hershey's
  Baking Chocolate, melted

Cream butter and sugar together; add cream and beat well. Gradually add melted baking chocolate, and beat thoroughly to reach spreading consistency. (Additional cream may be needed.) Makes 2 cups icing, or enough for an 8- or 9-inch layer cake.

All-American Apple Soufflé

Can't-fail soufflé, as delicious as it is different, from the label of the Dole Pineapple Slices can.

4 large apples
1 20-ounce can Dole
  Pineapple Slices, in
  syrup
1 envelope unflavored
  gelatine

¾ tsp. cinammon
¼ tsp. cardamom
1 tsp. lime juice
2 Tbs. finely chopped
  almonds
½ cup whipping cream

Pare, core and slice apples. Drain pineapple, reserving syrup. Cook apples and ½ cup pineapple syrup until soft. Sprinkle gelatine over remaining syrup and let stand 5 minutes. Stir into hot apple sauce until dissolved. Put apple mixture through food mill or purée in blender. Stir in spices, lime juice and almonds. Chill until mixture mounds on spoon. Whip cream and fold in. Stand pineapple slices around sides of 1½-quart soufflé dish. Pour in apple sauce mixture and chill until firm. Garnish with remaining pineapple slices and additional apple slices, if desired. Makes 4 to 6 servings.

Easy Apple Crisp

A great "quickie" from the Maypo Oatmeal box.

⅔ cup brown sugar, firmly packed
½ cup sifted flour
1 cup Maypo 30-Second Oatmeal

½ cup melted butter or margarine
1 can (1 lb., 4 ounces) apple pie filling

Mix dry ingredients together; blend in melted butter. Press two-thirds of mixture into a lightly buttered 8-inch square cake pan. Cover with pie filling. Sprinkle with remaining Maypo mixture. Bake in preheated 350°F. oven for 30 to 35 minutes, until lightly browned. Cool; cut into squares; serve topped with ice cream or whipped cream. Makes one 8-inch square.

Easy Cherry Pudding

Here's an old-fashioned favorite that appeared on cans of Stokely's Finest Red Sour Cherries thirty years back. Good enough for a party dinner, yet easy even for children to make. Serve warm with whipped cream if you like.

½ cup butter or margarine
1 cup sugar
1 cup flour
2 tsps. baking powder

¾ cup milk
1 1-lb. can Stokely's Finest Red Sour Pitted Cherries
½ cup sugar

In 9-inch square pan, melt butter or margarine. In bowl, combine next 4 ingredients. Mix until well blended. Pour over melted butter; do not stir. Pour undrained cherries over batter; do not stir. Sprinkle ½ cup sugar over cherries; do not stir. Bake at 325°F. for 1 hour. Makes 9 servings.

Crunchy Lemon Squares

Remember this one? I'll bet your mother does. It appeared on the Eagle Brand Condensed Milk can in 1947. It's still a popular and easy "company special" dessert.

1 cup quick oats, uncooked
1 cup flour
½ cup flaked coconut
½ cup coarsely chopped pecans
½ cup firmly packed light brown sugar
1 tsp. baking powder

½ cup butter or margarine, melted
1 can Eagle Brand Sweetened Condensed Milk
½ cup ReaLemon Reconstituted Juice
1 Tbs. grated lemon rind

Preheat oven to 350°F. (325°F. if using glass dish). In medium bowl, combine oats, flour, coconut, nuts, sugar, baking powder and butter; stir to form a crumbly mixture. Set aside. In medium bowl, combine sweetened condensed milk, lemon juice and rind. Pat half of crumb mixture evenly on bottom of 9 × 9-inch baking pan. Spread sweetened condensed milk mixture on top and sprinkle with remaining crumbs. Bake for 25 to 30 minutes or until lightly browned. Cool thoroughly before cutting. Makes 9 servings.

All-Time Favorite Puff Pudding

Although this interesting pudding did not appear on the Post Grape-Nuts package until 1952, it was originally developed for a book about Post Cereal's founder, C. W. Post, way back in 1926. It's a lovely dessert with a cakelike top layer and a creamy, lemony custard below.

¼ cup butter or margarine
½ cup sugar or honey
1 tsp. grated lemon rind

2 egg yolks
3 Tbs. lemon juice
2 Tbs. all-purpose flour

¼ cup Post Grape-Nuts
   Brand Cereal
1 cup milk

2 egg whites, stiffly
   beaten

Thoroughly cream butter with sugar and lemon rind. Add egg yolks; beat until light and fluffy. Blend in lemon juice, flour, cereal and milk. (Mixture will look curdled, but this will not affect finished product.) Fold in beaten egg whites. Pour into greased 1-quart baking dish; place the dish in pan of hot water. Bake at 325°F. for 1 hour and 15 minutes or until top springs back when lightly touched. When done, pudding has a cakelike layer on top with custard below. Serve warm or cold with cream or prepared whipped topping, if desired. Makes 4 to 6 servings.

Note: For individual puddings, pour mixture into five 5-ounce or four 6-ounce custard or soufflé cups. Bake for about 40 minutes.

Rice Pudding

Old-fashioned rice pudding. This recipe was a favorite even before Carolina Rice printed it on their box in the early 1940s. It's still the homey, familiar dessert everyone loves.

2 cups milk
½ cup uncooked Carolina
   Rice
¼ tsp. salt

3 egg yolks
3 Tbs. sugar
¾ cup heavy cream

Bring milk to boil; stir in rice and salt. Cook over hot water until milk is absorbed, about 30 minutes. Beat egg yolks with sugar and cream. Combine with rice mixture. Add raisins, if desired. Pour into baking dish. Bake in preheated 350°F. oven for 15 minutes, until top browns. Makes 8 servings.

A PAIR OF OLD-FASHIONED, WELL-LOVED PUDDINGS FROM GENERAL FOODS KITCHENS

Chocolate Tapioca Pudding

Here's a nourishing milk-and-egg dessert that's fast to fix and a favorite with chocolate lovers. Add instant coffee when you'd like a mocha flavor.

1 cup sugar
3 Tbs. Minute Tapioca
⅛ tsp. salt
3⅔ cups milk
1 egg, slightly beaten
1 tsp. vanilla

2 1-ounce squares Baker's Unsweetened Chocolate
2 to 3 tsps. Maxwell House Instant Coffee (optional)

Combine sugar, tapioca and salt in saucepan; stir in milk and egg. Let stand 5 minutes. Add chocolate and instant coffee. Cook and stir over medium heat until mixture comes to a full boil and chocolate is well blended, about 15 minutes. Remove from heat. Stir in vanilla. Cool for 20 minutes; stir. Chill. Serve with prepared Dream Whip Whipped Topping, if desired. Makes about 8 servings.

Heavenly Hash

Your little angels will sing for more of this heavenly treat with marshmallows and fruits floating amid clouds of pudding.

1 egg
⅓ cup sugar
2⅓ cups milk
3 Tbs. Minute Tapioca
¼ tsp. salt
1 8¼-ounce can crushed pineapple, drained

8 marshmallows, quartered
1 cup prepared Dream Whip Whipped Topping
2 Tbs. chopped maraschino cherries

Beat egg until thick and light in color. Gradually add sugar, beating thoroughly after each addition. Blend in milk, tapioca and salt. Let stand for 5 minutes. Pour into saucepan. Cook and stir over medium heat until mixture comes to a full boil. (Pudding thickens as it cools.) Cool for 20 minutes; fold in pineapple and marshmallows. Chill for at least 1 hour. Just before serving, fold in whipped topping and cherries. Makes 3½ cups or 6 or 7 servings.

Hot Curried Fruit

Here's a superb extra-easy dessert to end dinner with a flourish. It's from the Hiram Walker Cordials Entertaining Book.

Drain canned peaches, pears, pineapple, apricots and cherries. Layer in a Pyrex dish—first fruit, then dot with butter, sprinkle with brown sugar and curry powder, drizzle with Hiram Walker Blackberry Brandy. Make at least 3 layers. Bake one hour at 325°F.

  P.S. I like it swathed in sour cream.

Ribbon Icebox Dessert

An old-fashioned favorite, from Pet Milk's 1932 Cookbook.

1 30-ounce can fruit
  cocktail, drained,
  reserving liquid
2 3-ounce packages
  strawberry-flavored
  gelatine
30 graham crackers, each
  2½ inches square

½ cup butter or
  margarine, softened
2 cups powdered sugar
1 13-ounce can Pet
  Evaporated Milk
½ cup water

Heat 1½ cups fruit cocktail liquid to boiling (if not enough liquid, add water to make 1½ cups liquid). Add gelatine; stir until dissolved. Cool to room temperature. Place half of graham crackers in one layer on bottom of 13 × 9 × 2-inch pan. Beat butter until creamy; gradually beat in powdered sugar; add ⅓ cup evaporated milk, stirring in about 1 Tbs. at a time; beat well after each addition; spread over graham crackers in pan. Top with remaining graham crackers in a single layer. Refrigerate. Divide cooled gelatine into two equal portions. Stir 1⅓ cups evaporated milk into one portion. Chill until slightly thicker than unbeaten egg whites. Beat until fluffy. Spread over graham crackers. Refrigerate until firm. Stir ½ cup water and drained fruit cocktail into remaining dissolved gelatine. Pour over chilled gelatine–evaporated milk mixture. Chill until firm. Cut into squares and serve. Makes 12 servings.

HERSHEY'S CHOCOLATE SAUCES

- -

Here are two great chocolate sauces from the Hershey Company's 1934 Cookbook. Either one will transform just plain ice cream into a fabulous dessert. If you want to create something "extra special," try either one over poached pear or peach halves.

Chocolate Marshmallow Sauce

2 cups granulated sugar
1 cup boiling water
¼ cup Hershey's Cocoa
1 tsp. vanilla

½ cup shredded fresh marshallows
or
½ cup miniature marshmallows

Cook sugar and water in saucepan to 220°F. Remove from heat; stir in cocoa, vanilla and marshmallows until melted. Cool, without stirring, until bottom of pan just feels warm to hand. Beat to thicken and serve warm over ice cream. Makes 2 cups of sauce.

Chocolate Caramel Sauce

1 cup brown sugar, packed
Dash of salt
3 Tbs. water
¼ cup Hershey's Chocolate Flavored Syrup

1 Tbs. butter
1 Tbs. cornstarch
1 cup hot water
½ tsp. vanilla

Cook sugar and salt with 3 Tbs. water to a light caramel brown. Remove from heat; add chocolate syrup, butter and cornstarch mixed to a paste and 1 cup hot water. Cook over direct heat until thick (220°F.), for about 15 minutes; add vanilla. Serve with cottage pudding or other hot desserts. This sauce is very nice with ice cream. Makes 1 cup of sauce.

Sunkist Fresh Lemon Ice Cream

Leave it to a Californian to dream up this delicate, refreshingly different ice cream.

2 cups whipping cream or half-and-half
1 cup sugar
1 to 2 Tbs. fresh grated Sunkist Lemon Peel

⅓ cup fresh-squeezed Sunkist Lemon Juice

In large bowl, stir together cream and sugar until sugar is thoroughly dissolved. Mix in lemon peel and juice. Pour into 8-inch square pan, or directly into sherbet dishes or scooped-out lemon boats. Freeze several hours until firm. Garnish with lemon cartwheel twists, if desired. Makes about 1½ pints.

9.
Cookies
and
Candies

Anyone can whip up a batch of cookies. Recipes for them abound, but it takes something like a genius to dream up not only delicious morsels, but cookies so easy and fail-proof you just can't lose—even if you are a baker like my sister, whose intentions are good but whose skill at the stove, is, to put it politely, limited.

After the cookies come super candy recipes, beloved favorites, but favorites plotted by the experts to assure you that the fudge will be creamy, the peanut brittle snapping with crunchy sweetness, the English toffee just like the toffee someone sent to you from London. Last but not least, two all-time great popcorn treats: nostalgic souvenirs from your own childhood.

Cookies and candies are the jewels of the kitchen. A tray of still-warm cookies or a plate of just-made candy can indeed make life a little sweeter, a little more fun—and that's what it's all about, now, isn't it?

Ralston Crescents

"This recipe was sent in by a consumer about twenty years ago. It's still a favorite with our test kitchen home economists." This is exactly what the Ralston Purina Company told me, and after trying these cookies, I can see why.

1 cup butter or
 margarine
1 cup sifted confectioners'
 sugar
2 tsps. vanilla
2¼ cups sifted all-purpose
 flour

½ tsp. salt
1 cup uncooked Instant
 Ralston or ¾ cup
 uncooked Regular
 Ralston

Preheat oven to 325°F. Cream butter, adding sugar gradually. Add vanilla. Sift together flour and salt. Add to creamed mixture along with Ralston. Mix well. Shape dough by teaspoonfuls into 2½-inch crescents. Place on ungreased baking sheet. Bake for about 15 minutes or until edges are light brown. Roll in additional confectioners' sugar if desired. Makes about 5½ dozen cookies.

Barbara Uhlmann's Oatmeal Cookies

From Maypo Oatmeal, the very best oatmeal cookies.

¾ cup soft shortening
1 cup brown sugar, firmly packed
½ cup granulated sugar
1 egg
¼ cup water
1 tsp. vanilla

1 cup sifted flour
1 tsp. salt
½ tsp. baking soda
3 cups Maypo 30-Second Oatmeal
1 cup raisins
1 cup chopped nuts

Cream shortening and sugars. Add egg, water and vanilla; mix well. Sift dry ingredients together; add to creamed mixture and blend well. Stir in Maypo, raisins and nuts; mix thoroughly. Drop by teaspoonfuls onto lightly greased cookie sheet. Bake in preheated 350°F. oven for 12 to 15 minutes, or until tests done. Remove from pan; cool on rack. Makes about 5 dozen cookies.

Hiram Walker Amaretto Cookies

These are the most melt-in-the-mouth Italian-style cookies— more like macaroons actually. Brew up some espresso coffee and enjoy!

½ cup egg whites (3 eggs)
1¼ cup sugar
¼ tsp. salt
⅓ cup Hiram Walker
Amaretto liqueur

3¼ ounces flaked coconut
4 ounces almonds, finely
chopped

Beat egg whites until stiff. Then gradually beat in sugar, 1 Tbs. at a time, until stiff and glossy. Add salt. Gradually beat in Amaretto. Fold in coconut and almonds.

Foil-line cookie sheets. Drop mixture by heaping teaspoons onto foil. Bake at 325°F. for 20 minutes. Cool cookies on foil. Store in air-tight container. Makes 4 dozen.

Chocolate Date and Nut Bars

Rich, moist, chewy and delicious. You'll love these cookies from Hershey.

2 eggs
½ cup granulated sugar
½ cup sifted all-purpose
flour
1 tsp. baking powder
6 Tbs. Hershey's
Chocolate Flavored
Syrup

1 tsp. vanilla
½ cup walnut meats,
chopped
½ cup dates, chopped in
small pieces

Beat eggs thoroughly; gradually beat in sugar. Sift flour and baking powder; add to egg–sugar mixture; then add chocolate syrup, vanilla, nuts and dates. Beat mixture together; spread in a greased shallow 9 × 9-inch pan. Bake in a 350°F. oven for 25 minutes. Cool. Cut into 1 × 3-inch strips. Sprinkle with confectioners' sugar. Makes about 2 dozen bars.

Coconut Macaroons

These delicate-tasting, easy-to-make macaroons made their debut back in 1962 when the recipe appeared on Baker's Angel Flake Coconut packages. Despite their chewy goodness they are extra-low in calories, a sweet even the dieter can enjoy.

1⅓ cups (about) Baker's
    Angel Flake Coconut
⅓ cup sugar
2 Tbs. all-purpose flour

⅛ tsp. salt
2 egg whites
½ tsp. almond extract

Combine coconut, sugar, flour and salt in mixing bowl. Stir in egg whites and almond extract; mix well. Drop by teaspoonfuls onto lightly greased baking sheets. Garnish with candied cherry halves, if desired. Bake at 325°F. for 20 to 25 minutes, until edges of cookies are golden brown. Remove from baking sheets immediately. Makes about 1½ dozen.

Choco-Scotch Clusters

Some inspired genius in the Kellogg kitchen came up with this luscious combination of chocolate, butterscotch and peanut butter in the early 1940s.

1 6-ounce package semi-
    sweet chocolate morsels
1 6-ounce package
    butterscotch morsels

2 Tbs. peanut butter
4 cups Kellogg's Rice
    Krispies cereal

Melt chocolate, butterscotch morsels and peanut butter together in top section of double boiler over hot but not boiling water, or in heavy saucepan over very low heat, stirring constantly until well blended. Remove from heat. Add Rice Krispies; stir until well coated.

Drop by level measuring-tablespoon onto waxed paper or buttered baking sheets. Let stand in cool place until firm. Makes about 4 dozen Choco-Scotch Clusters, 1½ inches in diameter.

Note: Mixture may be pressed into buttered 9 × 9 × 2-inch square pan. Cut into squares when firm. Yields 3 dozen 1½ × 1½-inch Choco-Scotch Clusters.

Tiger Cookies

Kellogg's Tiger on the box inspired this great cookie recipe. It's been making chocolate fanciers happy for years.

1¾ cups all-purpose flour
½ tsp. baking soda
½ tsp. salt
1 cup margarine or butter, softened
1 cup sugar
2 eggs
1 tsp. vanilla

3 cups Kellogg's Sugar Frosted Flakes of Corn cereal, crushed to measure 1½ cups
1 6-ounce package semi-sweet chocolate morsels, melted

Stir together flour, soda and salt. Set aside. In large mixing bowl, beat margarine and sugar until light and fluffy. Add eggs and vanilla. Beat well. Add flour mixture, mixing until well combined. Stir in crushed Sugar Frosted Flakes of Corn cereal. Drizzle melted chocolate over dough. With knife, swirl melted chocolate gently through dough to achieve marbled appearance. Drop by rounded measuring-tablespoon onto ungreased baking sheets. Bake in 350°F. oven for about 12 minutes, until lightly browned. Remove immediately from baking sheets. Cool on wire racks. Makes about 5 dozen cookies.

Cherry Winks

These great Christmas cookies are from Kellogg. Moist, rich and festive, they have been a favorite for a generation.

2¼ cups all-purpose flour	1 cup finely cut pitted dates
2 tsps. baking powder	
½ tsp. salt	⅓ cup finely chopped candied red cherries
¾ cup margarine or butter, softened	
1 cup sugar	2⅔ cups Kellogg's Corn Flakes cereal, crushed to measure 1⅓ cups
2 eggs	
2 Tbs. milk	
1 tsp. vanilla	15 candied red cherries, cut into quarters
1 cup chopped nuts	

Stir together flour, baking powder and salt. Set aside. In large mixing bowl, beat margarine and sugar until light and fluffy. Add eggs. Beat well. Stir in milk and vanilla. Add flour mixture. Mix until well combined. Stir in nuts, dates and chopped cherries. Using level measuring-tablespoon, shape dough into balls. Roll in crushed Corn Flakes cereal. Place about 2 inches apart on greased baking sheets. Top each with cherry quarter. Bake in 375°F. oven for about 10 minutes, until lightly browned. Remove immediately from baking sheets. Cool on wire racks. Makes about 5 dozen.

Brownies

Two generations of American cooks have followed this recipe for brownies from the back of Baker's Unsweetened Chocolate package.

2 1-ounce squares Baker's Unsweetened Chocolate
⅓ cup soft butter or other shortening
⅔ cup all-purpose flour
½ tsp. Calumet Baking Powder
¼ tsp. salt
2 eggs
1 cup sugar
1 tsp. vanilla
½ cup chopped nuts

Melt chocolate with butter over low heat. Mix flour with baking powder and salt. Beat eggs well; then gradually beat in sugar. Blend in chocolate mixture and vanilla. Add flour mixture and mix well. Stir in nuts. Spread in greased 8-inch square pan. Bake at 350°F. for 25 minutes (for moist, chewy brownies); or about 30 minutes, or until cake tester inserted in center comes out clean (for cakelike brownies). Cool in pan; then cut into squares. Makes about 20 brownies.

Note: Recipe may be doubled; bake in greased 13 × 9 × 2-inch pan at 350°F. for 25 or 30 minutes, as directed. Makes about 40 brownies.

Famous Oatmeal Cookies

Quaker Oats first printed this cookie recipe on their oats package in 1955 but I suspect it was a favorite even before that.

¾ cup shortening, soft
1 cup firmly packed brown sugar
½ cup granulated sugar
1 egg
¼ cup water

1 tsp. vanilla	½ tsp. baking soda
1 cup sifted all-purpose flour	3 cups uncooked Quaker Oats
1 tsp. salt	

Beat together shortening, sugars, egg, water and vanilla until creamy. Sift together flour, salt and soda; add to creamed mixture; blend. Stir in oats. Drop by teaspoonfuls onto greased cookie sheets. Bake in preheated 350°F. oven for 12 to 15 minutes. Makes 5 dozen cookies.

Toll House Cookies With Variations

Remember Empress Eugenie hats? If you do, you were around in 1939 when the Nestlé Company first printed this now famous cookie recipe on their Semi-Sweet Chocolate Morsels package.

2¼ cups unsifted all-purpose flour*	1 tsp. vanilla
1 tsp. baking soda	2 eggs
1 tsp. salt	1 package (12 ounces) Nestlé Semi-Sweet Real Chocolate Morsels
1 cup butter, softened	
¾ cup sugar	1 cup chopped nuts
¾ cup firmly packed brown sugar	

Preheat oven to 375°F. Combine flour, baking soda and salt in a small bowl; set aside. Combine butter, sugars, and vanilla extract in large bowl; beat until creamy. Beat in eggs. Gradually add flour mixture; blend well. Stir in Nestlé Semi-Sweet Real Chocolate Morsels and nuts. Drop by rounded teaspoonfuls onto ungreased

* For Whole-Wheat Toll House Cookies, substitute whole-wheat flour for all or half of all-purpose flour.

cookie sheets. Bake at 375°F. for 8 to 10 minutes. Makes 100 2-inch cookies.

Variations: Omit nuts and substitute one of the following: 4 cups crisp ready-to-eat cereal; 2 cups chopped dates; 1 Tbs. grated orange rind; or 2 cups raisins.

Corn Flakes Macaroons

Kellogg developed these chewy cookies over twenty years ago, but cooks all over the country still write in for "that marvelous macaroon recipe."

4 egg whites	1 cup chopped pecans
¼ tsp. cream of tartar	1 cup shredded coconut
1 tsp. vanilla	3 cups Kellogg's Corn
1⅓ cups sugar	Flakes cereal

In large mixing bowl, beat egg whites until foamy. Stir in cream of tartar and vanilla. Gradually add sugar, beating until stiff and glossy. Fold in pecans, coconut and Corn Flakes cereal. Drop by rounded measuring-tablespoon onto well-greased baking sheets. Bake in 325°F. oven for about 20 minutes or until lightly browned. Remove immediately from baking sheets. Cool on wire racks. Makes about 3 dozen macaroons.

Variation: Merry Macaroons: Fold in ½ cup crushed peppermint candy with pecans, coconut and cereal.

Magic Cookie Bars

Children have delighted in this recipe ever since it appeared on the Eagle Brand Condensed Milk can light-years ago. As easy for kids to make as it is for them to eat.

½ cup butter or margarine	1½ cups graham cracker crumbs

1 can Eagle Brand
Sweetened Condensed
Milk
1 6-ounce package semi-
sweet chocolate
morsels

1 3-ounce can flaked
coconut
1 cup chopped nuts

Preheat oven to 350°F. (or 325°F. if you use a glass dish). In 13 × 9-inch baking pan, melt butter. Sprinkle crumbs over butter. Pour sweetened condensed milk evenly over crumbs. Top evenly with chocolate morsels, coconut, and nuts; press down gently. Bake for 25 to 30 minutes or until lightly browned. Cool thoroughly before cutting. Makes 24 bars.

Crisp Peanut Butter Cookies

One of the best peanut butter cookie recipies, a long-time favorite from the Skippy Peanut Butter label.

2½ cups unsifted flour
1 tsp. baking powder
1 tsp. baking soda
1 tsp. salt
1 cup corn oil margarine
1 cup Skippy Creamy or
Super Chunk Peanut
Butter

1 cup sugar
1 cup firmly packed
brown sugar
2 eggs, beaten
1 tsp. vanilla

Stir together flour, baking powder, baking soda and salt. In large bowl with mixer at medium speed beat margarine and peanut butter until smooth. Beat in sugars until blended. Beat in eggs and vanilla. Add flour mixture and beat well. If necessary, chill dough. Shape into 1-inch balls. Place on ungreased cookie sheet 2 inches apart. Flatten with floured fork, making crisscross pattern. Bake in 350°F. oven for 12 minutes or until lightly browned. Cool on wire rack. Makes 6 dozen 2-inch cookies.

Peanut Butter Sandwich Cookies: Follow basic recipe. Spread bottoms of half of baked cookies with peanut butter; top with remaining cookies. Makes about 3 dozen cookies.

Jelly Thumbprint Cookies: Follow basic recipe. Instead of flattening with fork, press small indentation in each with thumb. While still warm press again with thumb. Cool. Fill indentation with jelly or jam.

Peanut Butter Refrigerator Cookies: Follow basic recipe. Shape into 2 rolls 1½-inches in diameter. Wrap in plastic wrap and refrigerate. Slice into ¼-inch thick slices. Bake as directed. Makes about 8 dozen cookies.

Peanut Butter Crackles: Follow basic recipe. Roll in sugar before placing on cookie sheet; do not flatten. Bake as directed for 15 to 18 minutes. Immediately press chocolate candy kiss firmly into top of each cookie (cookie will crack around edges).

Marshmallow Treats

As long as there are children, these easy marshmallow "cookies-candies" will be favorites.

¼ cup margarine or butter
1 10-ounce package marshmallows or 4 cups miniature marshmallows

5 cups Kellogg's Rice Krispies cereal

Melt margarine in large saucepan over low heat. Add marshmallows and stir until completely melted. Cook over low heat for 3 minutes longer, stirring constantly. Remove from heat. Add Rice Krispies cereal. Stir until well coated. Using buttered spatula or waxed paper, press mixture evenly into buttered 13 × 9 × 2-inch pan. Cut into 2-inch squares when cool. Makes 24 squares.

Note: Best results are obtained when using fresh marshmallows.

Variations: To make thicker squares, press warm mixture into buttered 9 × 9 × 2-inch pan.

Marshmallow Crème Treats: About 2 cups marshmallow crème may be substituted for marshmallows. Add to melted margarine and stir until well blended. Cook over low heat for about 5 minutes longer, stirring constantly. Remove from heat. Proceed as directed in step 2 above.

Peanut Treats: Add 1 cup salted cocktail peanuts with the cereal.

Peanut Butter Treats: Stir ¼ cup peanut butter into marshmallow mixture just before adding cereal.

Raisin Treats: Add 1 cup seedless raisins with cereal.

Cocoa Krispies Cereal Treats: 6 cups Cocoa Krispies cereal may be substituted for 5 cups Rice Krispies cereal.

Magic Marshmallow Crescent Puffs

These sweet puffs have become a favorite of many. They were the best of the twentieth Pillsbury Bake-Off contest in 1968. The recipe for them has been requested over and over again.

¼ cup sugar
1 tsp. cinnamon
2 8-ounce cans Pillsbury Refrigerated Quick Crescent Dinner Rolls

16 large marshmallows
¼ cup margarine or butter, melted
¼ cup chopped nuts, if desired

Glaze:

½ cup powdered sugar
2 to 3 tsps. milk
½ tsp. vanilla

Heat oven to 375°F. Combine sugar and cinnamon. Separate crescent dough into 16 triangles. Dip a marshmallow in melted margarine; roll in sugar-cinnamon mixture. Place marshmallow on shortest side of triangle. Fold corners over marshmallow and roll to opposite point, completely covering marshmallow and pinching edges of dough to seal. Dip in melted margarine and place margarine side down in deep muffin cup. Repeat with remaining marshmallows. Place pan on foil or cookie sheet during baking to guard against spillage. Bake at 375°F. for 10 to 15 minutes or until golden brown. Immediately remove from pans.

Glaze: Combine Glaze ingredients; drizzle over warm rolls. Sprinkle with nuts. Makes 16 rolls.

Note: To reheat, wrap in foil; heat at 375°F. for 5 to 10 minutes.

High Altitude: No change.

Oatmeal Carmelitas

The eighteenth Pillsbury Bake-Off contest gave us this bar cookie that is a favorite in homes across America. It will become your favorite, too. Who doesn't like a caramel taste?

8 ounces (about 32) light candy caramels
5 Tbs. light cream or evaporated milk
1 cup Pillsbury's Best All Purpose or Unbleached Flour*
1 cup quick-cooking rolled oats
¾ cup firmly packed brown sugar
½ tsp. baking soda
¼ tsp. salt
¾ cup margarine or butter, melted
1 6-ounce package milk chocolate or semi-sweet chocolate chips
½ cup chopped pecans

Melt caramels in cream in top of double boiler. Cool slightly. Set aside. Heat oven to 350°F. Lightly spoon flour into measuring cup; level off. In a large bowl, combine flour and remaining ingredients except chocolate chips and pecans. Press half of crumbs in bottom of ungreased 11 × 7- or 9-inch square pan. Bake at 350°F. for 10 minutes.

Remove from oven. Sprinkle with chocolate chips and pecans. Spread carefully with caramel mixture. Sprinkle with remaining crumb mixture. Bake for 15 to 20 minutes longer, until golden brown. Chill 1 to 2 hours. Cut into bars. Makes 2 dozen bars.

Note: ¾ cup caramel ice cream topping combined with 3 Tbs. flour may be substituted for the melted caramel mixture.

High Altitude: Above 3500 feet, bake at 375°F.

* If using Pillsbury's Best Self-Rising Flour, omit soda and salt.

English Toffee

One of the very first recipes featured in Blue Diamond Almond advertising was this super toffee, not only "the real thing" but also a snap to make.

1 cup Blue Diamond Blanched Slivered Almonds, toasted
1 cup butter or margarine

1 cup sugar
⅓ cup (2 ounces) semi-sweet chocolate bits

Chop almonds and spread ½ cup in bottom of buttered 7 × 11-inch pan. Combine butter and sugar in heavy skillet; cook, stirring until boiling point is reached. Boil over medium heat, stirring constantly to soft-crack stage, 270° to 280°F. Pour carefully over almonds. Let stand for about 10 minutes until top is set. Sprinkle chocolate over top of candy. When heat of candy has melted chocolate, smooth with spatula. Sprinkle remaining almonds over chocolate. Let stand until cold. Break into squares. Makes about 1½ pounds.

Peanut Brittle

For many years this has been a favorite recipe from the Karo label. It's a sure-fire success, time after time!

1 cup Karo Light or Dark Corn Syrup
1 cup sugar
¼ cup water

2 Tbs. corn oil margarine
1½ cups salted peanuts
1 tsp. baking soda

Grease 1 baking sheet. In heavy 3-quart saucepan stir together corn syrup, sugar, water and margarine. Cook over medium heat, stirring constantly, until sugar is dissolved and mixture comes to boil. Continue cooking without stirring until temperature reaches 280°F. on candy thermometer, or until small amount dropped into very cold water separates into threads which are hard but not brittle. Gradually stir in peanuts; continue cooking, stirring frequently, until temperature reaches 300°F., or until small amount of mixture dropped into very cold water separates into threads which are hard and brittle. Remove from heat; stir in baking soda. Immediately pour mixture onto baking sheet. Spread mixture evenly to edges with greased metal spatula. Cool. Break into pieces. Makes about 1½ pounds.

Magic French Fudge

Fool-proof, fail-proof, and delicious!

3 6-oz. pkgs. semi-sweet chocolate morsels	Dash salt
1 8-ounce can Eagle Brand Sweetened Condensed Milk	1½ tsps. vanilla ½ cup chopped nuts (optional)

In top of double boiler, melt chocolate over boiling water, stirring occasionally. Remove from heat; stir in sweetened condensed milk, salt, vanilla, and nuts. Spread mixture evenly into waxed-paper-lined 8 × 8-inch baking pan. Chill for 2 hours or until firm. Turn fudge onto cutting board; peel off paper and cut into squares. Tightly cover any leftovers! Makes about 1¾ pounds.

Chocolate Chip-Peanut Butter Fudge

If you love fudge, you'll love this recipe from the package of Hershey's Milk Chocolate Chips.

2 cups sugar
⅔ cup milk
2 Tbs. light corn syrup
1 Tbs. butter
1 tsp. vanilla

½ cup peanut butter
1 5¾-ounce package Hershey's Milk Chocolate Chips

Combine sugar, milk and corn syrup in a heavy 3-quart saucepan; bring to a boil, stirring constantly, until mixture boils. Continue boiling without stirring to the soft-ball stage (234°F.). Remove from heat. Add butter without stirring; cool to lukewarm (110°F.).

Add vanilla and peanut butter; beat until mixture begins to thicken and lose its gloss. (Watch carefully; this fudge has a short beating time.) Quickly add chocolate pieces, and turn into buttered 8 × 8 × 2-inch pan. While warm, mark into squares. Cool until firm, then cut as marked. Makes about 3 dozen squares.

Chocolate Pecan Pralines

From Hershey's 1934 book the most delicious pralines I've ever eaten—and I lived for many years in New Orleans, where pralines were born.

1 cup sugar
1 cup light brown sugar or maple sugar, packed
½ cup light cream
¼ tsp. salt
1 tsp. vanilla

2 1-ounce squares Hershey's Baking Chocolate
1 Tbs. butter
1 cup coarsely chopped pecans

Combine sugars, cream and salt in a large saucepan. Cook over medium heat, stirring constantly, to 228°F. on candy thermometer. Remove from heat, and add baking chocolate broken into small pieces, butter and pecans. Return to heat; stirring constantly, cook to soft-ball stage (234°F.). Remove from heat; flavor with vanilla; cool for 5 minutes. Beat for 10 to 15 seconds or until slightly thickened. Quickly drop candy by large spoonfuls onto greased plates (or waxed paper). If mixture becomes too thick to drop, stir in a tablespoonful of hot water. Makes about 2 dozen pieces.

SMITH FAMILY FAVORITES

Back in 1914 Cloid C. Smith established the American Pop Corn Company with Jolly Time Pop Corn, a family-owned business to this day. Both of these pop corn recipes, "Smith Family Favorites," have appeared on the Jolly Time label— the pop corn balls in 1920; the caramel corn, 1929.

Pop Corn Balls

6 quarts popped Jolly
  Time Pop Corn
1 cup sugar
⅓ cup light corn syrup

⅓ cup water
¼ cup butter
¾ tsp. salt
¾ tsp. vanilla

Keep pop corn hot in 300°F. oven. Stir and cook sugar, corn syrup, water, butter and salt until sugar is dissolved. Continue cooking without stirring to 270°F., or until syrup forms a brittle ball in cold water. Add vanilla. Pour syrup slowly over popped corn, mixing well to coat every kernel. Grease hands with butter before shaping in balls. Makes 12 medium-sized balls.

Note: Nuts, candied cherries or raisins may be added before combining with syrup.

Baked Caramel Corn

1 cup (2 sticks) butter or margarine
2 cups firmly packed brown sugar
½ cup light or dark corn syrup

1 tsp. salt
½ tsp. baking soda
1 tsp. vanilla
6 quarts popped Jolly Time Pop Corn

Melt butter; stir in brown sugar, corn syrup and salt. Bring to a boil, stirring constantly. Boil without stirring for 5 minutes. Remove from heat; stir in soda and vanilla. Gradually pour over popped corn, mixing well. Turn into 2 large shallow baking pans. Bake in 250°F oven for 1 hour, stirring every 15 minutes. Remove from oven; cool completely. Break apart. Makes about 5 quarts Caramel Corn.

Index